The Greatest Story
Ever Told

The Greatest Show
Ever Told

The Greatest Story Ever Told

Bear Grylls

HODDER &
STOUGHTON

First published in Great Britain in 2025 by Hodder Faith
An imprint of John Murray Press

13

Copyright © Bear Grylls 2025

The right of Bear Grylls to be identified as the Author of the Work
has been asserted by him in accordance with the Copyright,
Designs and Patents Act 1988.

A CIP catalogue record for this title is available from the British Library

Hardback ISBN 978 1 399 82014 1
ebook ISBN 978 1 399 82015 8
Christmas ed. ISBN 978 1 399 83556 5
audio ISBN 978 1 399 82956 4

Typeset in Celeste ST by Palimpsest Book Production Limited,
Falkirk, Stirlingshire

Printed and bound by CPI (UK) Ltd, Croydon CR0 4YY

John Murray Press policy is to use papers that are natural, renewable and
recyclable products and made from wood grown in sustainable forests. The
logging and manufacturing processes are expected to conform to the
environmental regulations of the country of origin.

Carmelite House
50 Victoria Embankment
London EC4Y 0DZ

www.hodderfaith.com

John Murray Press, part of Hodder & Stoughton Limited
An Hachette UK company

The authorised representative in the EEA is Hachette Ireland,
8 Castlecourt Centre, Dublin 15, D15 XTP3, Ireland
(email: info@hbgi.ie)

Contents

This is the true story about a man from Galilee who lived some two thousand years ago. It is told through the eyes of the people who knew him best: a mother, a sceptic, a fisherman, a friend and a woman from Magdala.

Most died for their conviction that these events occurred in all their fullness.

Many consider what you're about to read:

The Greatest Story Ever Told. . .

*I will tell things that have been secrets
since the world was made.
Matthew 13:35*

ANCIENT PROPHETS AND Far Eastern mystics had foretold this man's life for many hundreds of years.

A coming king who would hold the very keys to the kingdom of heaven itself.

Yet into first-century Yehuda – a region of the Roman Empire – an impoverished child was born, who fled with his family as a refugee to Egypt but then returned and worked as a simple carpenter and stonemason. He eventually became a renegade. To others a redeemer.

This man was born into a time of turmoil, into a people who lived under the fear and control of one of the most brutal and expansive empires ever to have existed.

He owned seemingly nothing, yet many claimed he had power over every force of good and evil.

How he lived – his words, his actions – altered the world forever.

Many called him Master, yet others labelled him a 'glutton and a drunkard'. Others, whose lives were reportedly healed and changed by him, called him the Lamb of God and Light of the World. Those who were threatened by him were convinced he was the devil himself.

Yet those who spent the most time with him, often the outcasts and forgotten, washed his feet with tears of joy.

His local name was Yeshua.

The literal translation is: 'He who saves.'

PROLOGUE

Yerushalayim

C. AD 33

Three days after the torture and execution

'TELL ME WHAT you're discussing,' the traveller asked nonchalantly as he increased his pace, so that he was now walking alongside the two.

The man seemed not to have a care in the world.

'Why are you so downhearted?' the traveller enquired.

Clopas rebuked the man. 'You must be the only person in all the country who hasn't heard what's been going on.' He spat on the ground and wiped his mouth with the sleeve of his cloak.

'We had so hoped and prayed that a Messiah would prevail against these Romans.' He paused. 'Today we taste no victory. Only bitter defeat.'

The friend with him added quietly, 'It is true. These Romans aren't leaving this land any time soon.'

The small group continued to walk the dusty road together. The traveller's cloak and hood covered his head, and in one of his rough hands he rolled some pebbles between his fingers as he walked. He seemed to struggle to contain his zeal.

This moment had long been coming.

Finally, he could hold himself back no longer.

'How slow you are to believe all that the prophets have spoken!'

There was an urgency and intensity in his voice.

'Did not the Messiah have to suffer these things?' He paused for effect. 'And *then* enter his glory?'

The two companions turned to look at the man walking beside them.

'I don't understand,' Clopas replied.

The traveller shielded his face and kept walking.

The two companions quickened their pace to keep up with the man.

And there on that road from Yerushalayim to Hammath, with the sun slowly setting in the west, the traveller began to explain to them the Scriptures.

He told them all that the prophets had foretold about the Messiah and Saviour.

And their hearts felt on fire within themselves.

PART ONE

Myriam, Mother

Nazaret,
AROUND 33 YEARS EARLIER

A small village in the wild hill country of Galilee, made up of around five hundred subsistence farmers and construction workers.

1

The Light

I WAS ONLY sixteen years old, but I knew enough to know whether I was dreaming or awake.

I sat bolt upright, instantly alert.

There was a presence in my room. I knew it. I could feel it. I looked around, terrified, but could see nothing.

I held my breath. It was like I could feel something was about to happen, but I didn't know what.

And then suddenly the room exploded with light, and I grabbed my bed covers, hiding my face in terror.

What was happening?

Something inside told me not to scream – not to be afraid. I tried to calm myself, but I couldn't.

The light persisted and seemed to penetrate even through my blanket. I tried to breathe.

Then I just knew – that the presence, the light, was not here to harm me. It was pure and good. And my fear turned to excitement. Then I started to tremble.

I didn't know what was happening.

In my young life I had always tried my best to be good, to do what was right, to be loyal, dutiful and kind. But nothing had ever prepared me that one day the light of heaven would shine upon me.

I could do nothing except hide my face and pray.

After what felt like an eternity, but was probably only several seconds, I could sense someone was there. In my room. And then I heard a voice.

I had never heard a voice quite like it. Pure and full of love and power.

It spoke the sweetest words I had ever heard spoken.

'You are truly blessed. The Lord is with you.'

Slowly, I pulled the covers away from my eyes and looked up.

There in front of me – brighter than the brightest star in the night sky – was an angel in human form. Twice as tall as any person I'd ever seen.

The angel was smiling. Radiating love and light.

My eyes were so wide, they felt like saucers. I could not even blink. My mouth was dry, and I felt it drop open.

Then the angel smiled, raised a hand and spoke again right to me: 'You are truly blessed. The Lord is with you.'

The walls of our house might have been made of mud and straw but it was like I could see right through them and out into the great beyond. The light filled everywhere. And it seemed to sing. Sweet sounds that merged with the words that the angel spoke to me.

He didn't just tell me that I was blessed and that the Lord was with me, but went on to tell me I was pregnant, that the child would be called Yeshua, the Son of the Most High, and that his kingdom would never end.

Suddenly this fear began to rise inside me once more, and I asked the angel how this could be since I was a virgin.

The angel told me that nothing was impossible for God, and that my cousin Elizabeth, who was barren, would also soon give birth to a child.

My heart leapt within me. For us both.

Then the light intensified even further and, just like that, the angel departed. I was left alone.

My body was still shaking – with the sheer shock and excitement. But I remember I was no longer terrified.

After some time sitting there, I noticed I was cold. The embers from the night's fire were still warm in the hearth, so I gathered them gently together and blew them into a small flame.

I sat there, staring at the small flickering fire, for a long time.

I prayed without words. Like I had never prayed before.

I could not believe what had just happened. And I dared not tell anyone at first.

I mean, who would believe me? Really?

One thing I knew: my life would never be the same again.

2

My Song

THE MONTHS THAT followed were like the beginnings of a storm.

At times, I felt a sense of unbridled excitement. Like when I first visited my cousin Elizabeth – to ask if she had experienced anything similar. But before I could even get the question out, she told me everything that had happened to her.

Her husband, Zechariah, had also been visited by an angel. By this same light and power. I was so happy that I was not alone in all this craziness.

Sometimes, though, I felt the fear. What would people say? How would they react when my pregnancy started to show? After all, I was yet to be formally married to Yosef. I knew that people would start gossiping, and the fear tasted bitter in my mouth.

But what I dreaded most was telling Yosef. I feared he would think me a liar, an adulterer. Deluded. And I would be cast out.

I was more terrified of how he would react than I ever had been seeing that angel.

But Yosef proved to be a kind man. And I thank God every day that he professed to understand and to believe me. He promised he would protect and stay with me.

But at times I doubted myself and I feared he would soon change his mind. So far, he had guarded me from public disgrace – but I feared he would have in mind to divorce me quietly once my child was born.

Men's good intentions can sometimes fall away when they are scared.

And my genuine fear was whether Yosef would still be by my side when the baby came.

There were moments of calm though too. Days when I would pause whatever I was doing, rest my hand on my stomach and breathe.

'Hope. Trust. Pray.' It was all I could do.

Time passed. And little by little, I found myself repeating certain phrases, over and over. They felt silly at first, but I didn't care. They just kept coming back to me. Over and over. It helped to say them often. Sometimes I would even sing them to myself:

> I'm bursting with good news!
> I'm the most fortunate woman on earth . . .

I had no idea at the time, but this song became like oxygen to me. I repeated it hourly sometimes. I would breathe it in, and breathe it out.

Some weeks later, Yosef came rushing in early to see me. His face was alive with light and excitement. He could hardly get the words out. He himself had seen the angel. And clear as day, he had heard the most beautiful and reassuring words: that he was to marry me, that he must not fear – that my child was indeed from God.

That changed everything for us. I could now finally trust him and let my fears go. We had each other, and the truth of not one but three angelic appearances, reminding us that we were not just dreaming.

We talked non-stop about everything, in humble disbelief and wonder.

Life carried on like this for months and the initial storm inside of me subsided. Yosef and I married, my belly got big and I knew that the birth would happen soon.

I was peaceful about it, until one morning Yosef woke me up and told me the news.

3

The Journey

YOSEF HAD ALWAYS been a man of few words, measuring them carefully – just like he did with his tools at work.

'You know that the town has had word of a Roman census,' he announced quietly. 'They are demanding everyone returns and registers in their town of birth.'

He paused.

'It has come at a hard time, I know. But we must do what is asked. We have no choice.'

I let the words sink in.

Then he added: 'Myriam, we must leave Nazaret and go to Beit Lechem.'

He paused.

I was silent. Thinking.

'You never know . . . it could even be a fresh start. Away from this sleepy town and all the chatter. We can start our life together . . . just you, me and our baby?'

He looked at me, waiting for a response.

He continued: 'I still have cousins there. They should give us shelter.'

'When would we have to go?' I finally replied to him.

'Soon. Before you give birth.'

I took a slow breath, picturing the long journey. Moving was hard for me now. I had no idea how we would manage. But I did not question.

'We must do what is right. And take things day by day.'

But I was worried. It was so far from my family and from my home.

There was so much for me to process.

But within a few days, we set off.

We told few people, beyond our close family, of our plans. It felt better that way. The last few months had been hard on Yosef. All the gossip as my tummy had grown.

Maybe it was time to leave, and to cleave to my husband in whatever way that meant. Wherever it would lead us.

Back when I had visited Elizabeth, I was only just pregnant. I practically ran along the dusty coastal trade road that runs south towards Yerushalayim. Now, with the baby straining within me, I was slower than an old mule. Every step felt exhausting.

The journey which should have taken four days stretched closer to five, and the longer it went on the quieter Yosef became. He was worried, I could tell. I did the one thing I could do to help. I shared my song with him, my prayer. I had new words by then too:

> God embraced us. . .
> He remembered us. . .
> Exactly as he promised!

Yosef smiled when I finished. Then he asked me to sing it again.

By the time we turned and put the sea at our backs and headed up into the Yehudan hills, it was my turn to grow quiet. I was in more pain now, but not just from the walking. I knew that the time was getting close, that it would not be too long before I would have to stop and let the birth happen.

Wherever we were.

We pressed on as fast as I could possibly walk. Or waddle.

It was dusk when we arrived in the bustling town of Beit Lechem.

Even though it was almost night-time, the village was filled with movement and people. It seemed everyone was in a hurry.

We pushed anxiously through the crowds and eventually we were directed to the home of Yosef's cousins. As soon as the door opened it was obvious that we'd arrived at a bad time. It was late. The oil lamps had been lit and the animals put away into the small stable shelter at the side of the home.

I noticed at once that the house was full of people, and Yosef's relatives looked worried to see us standing there in such a state.

They tried to hide their awkwardness and invited us inside, but one of the little children soon confirmed our worst fears.

'Mama, there's no room for anyone else to stay here!' said the little girl, her face poking out from behind her mother's skirt. 'Where will you put them?'

Our hearts sank.

Beit Lechem was one of the final villages on the pilgrimage route. With so many people heading to Yerushalayim, every home was full of visitors from out of town. If we couldn't stay with Yosef's family, there was truly nowhere else to go.

I'd never met Yosef's cousins before, but they proved faithful and kind, and I thanked God – especially as I was soon to go into labour.

The family said we could stay, and that they would make some space. They moved the larger animals out from the small shelter at the side of the house and brought in fresh straw. A small donkey and some goats remained inside – but they would provide some warmth and protection.

I liked that.

The stable was small, dark and dirty, but it would do – and we were so thankful.

The family bustled around, trying to make this small animal shelter a little more homely and comfortable. But I was simply too tired even to speak.

They gave Yosef a few dried figs and some milk for him to give to me, then they left us to ourselves as they had much else to attend to.

I didn't mind. I was just grateful to lie down anywhere.

For a moment, the immediate struggle abated. I was safe.

I lay there and exhaled. All memories of angels or journeys or ancient Scriptures being fulfilled were gone. I just needed to rest. I closed my eyes, tried to pray and be calm.

'I'm ready to serve,' I said. 'Let it be, just as you say.'

4

The Outcasts

I WAS FEELING overwhelmed by everything. It had been a whirlwind – and I was so exhausted.

I slept for a few peaceful hours. Then early the next morning the contractions started, and I was woken with an agonising start that made me gulp with pain. I buried my head into my shawl and prayed for help.

In that corner of the stable, surrounded by the warmth and smell of the animals, I eventually gave birth to our precious son. I dozed in a dream-like state, where all I remember was a sense that the presence of God was upon me.

Nestled in the straw on top of the dry mud floor, I held my baby close and breathed in his scent and wrapped his small hand in my fingers.

That was all I needed.

I'd never known such peace and joy. I'd never felt so much happiness. Watching the baby sleep, then watching him wake, staring back at me with eyes that shone pure love, it was a taste of heaven.

The next day, the realities of life hit me hard. The frantic comings and goings of this bustling village meant that it was impossible to rest for long. The door never seemed to remain closed for more than a minute.

At times of holy festivals, trade never ceased. Even though the stable was warm, you couldn't escape the smell and the squalor. It was unlike anything I'd experienced. Blood, urine and dung from the slaughtered creatures, sold to pilgrims, flowed in the roads and ditches at this time of year. And the noise of so many travellers was all-consuming. Yet inside with the domestic animals, I felt safe.

I lay back and closed my eyes.

The next night, I woke up just before midnight, knowing something was wrong.

I could hear men were crowding outside the doorway. The women of the house were watching anxiously. Yosef was up and with them. The men were strangers, and when I heard Yosef speak, his voice sounded tense.

Panic bit into me and I sat up to check on the baby. He was sleeping soundly, unaware of anything.

'Don't worry,' one of Yosef's female cousins whispered quietly to me round the doorway. 'Everything is fine. It's just some people asking questions.'

'Who are they?' I replied.

'Shepherds?' she said, shaking her head. 'I think they want directions.'

I tried to listen as the men talked. Their voices raised. It was a rough dialect. Hard to understand. I couldn't make out much of the conversation so I moved myself closer. Then I heard one of the shepherds speak plain and clear for all to hear.

'I'm telling you this is the right place. I swear it.'

The shepherd then took a deep breath and spoke in a softer tone. 'It's exactly like they said it would be.'

I shuffled even closer so I could get a glimpse through the gap in the walls. The shepherds were all Yosef's age or older, but they sounded like a bunch of excited little boys. They were wide-eyed and eager to get inside. I couldn't help feel a surge of excitement in my heart.

But confusion too. For months Yosef and I had kept the secret about our baby to ourselves. We hadn't told anyone. Yet now there were these people outside who appeared to know. But how? And why shepherds?

These were certainly not prophets who were standing at our door. They were outcasts, the sort who normally would be told to stay outside after working so long with the animals.

I heard one of them curse to his friend beside him. Frustrated at the waiting.

Definitely not prophets, I smiled to myself.

It had been four hundred years since God had chosen to

send any messenger to speak with his people. There had been no prophets since Malachi, and nobody had seen any angels since Daniel in Babylon. Yet in the space of a few weeks, Yosef, myself and Zechariah had all been visited by an angel.

All of us had been left stunned; Zechariah so much so that he couldn't even talk until his son Yohanan had been born.

So, who was I to question the shepherds?

I didn't care that it was late, and I didn't care that they were dirty. I just knew that these outsiders, these most unlikely people, had been led here – to this baby in my arms.

I had a sense that this moment had somehow been beautifully planned. And this plan included all kinds of people – even unknowns like myself and outcasts like the shepherds.

Just then, the door opened, shaking me back to reality. Yosef edged in, bringing our visitors behind him. He looked half apprehensive, half excited.

There must have been at least ten shepherds. I covered my face, in respect, yet I could still smell them. No one said so much as a word. The shepherds looked awkwardly at me, then at each other and then at the baby in my arms.

They were all pressing forward, trying to get as close as they could to see the child.

The moment the first shepherd got close enough, I lowered my veil and peeled back the cloths that covered my baby. The man started silently to weep. Tears of pure joy rolled down his rugged, bearded, lined face.

One by one the others all shuffled forward, staring at us in that crowded corner of the lower room, surrounded by the animals.

'It's true,' said one. He was younger than the others. 'Just like the angels said.'

'Angels?' I asked him eagerly. 'There were more than one?'

He stared at me. His voice was cracked and whispered, like he was using it for the first time.

'Many angels.' He looked nervously around at his friends. 'A whole army of them. Enough to fill the sky. All because of this baby. He's the Messiah, isn't he?'

It was my turn to weep. It was just as we had been instructed. It was beginning to happen. I could feel it.

Then, excitedly, we told the shepherds that we had been told to call the child Yeshua.

It means: 'He who saves'.

5

Secret No More

I CAN'T TELL you how long we all stayed like that, the shepherds pressed in on all sides. It might have been hours. But eventually they left.

Once they were gone, I looked around and realised that Yosef's cousins had been in the room all the time. They'd seen and heard everything. And now it was their turn to stare in amazement and ask their questions.

Were the shepherds telling the truth?

Had we seen angels too?

Was little Yeshua really the Messiah, the one the Scriptures talked about? But how?

We tried our best to answer them, fumbling the words. Many of them looked confused, as if Yosef and I were crazy. I understood how they felt. My head was just as full of questions.

Ever since this all began, part of me had been wondering whether we'd really got it right. But knowing now that the shepherds had also been visited by angels, I dared even more to believe. Shepherds were not the sort of people known for hysterics, and that helped reassure me I wasn't dreaming.

Yosef reminded me of the Scriptures, and how such a great host of angels had never been seen before by humans.

Yet for this? For our child? An army of angels had appeared. Not only that, but they had been sent to exactly the right house at exactly the right time to find us.

The shepherds' visit changed everything for me. This wasn't just our secret anymore.

When everyone had finally left us alone, I felt even more

tired than I had on that last day of the journey from Nazaret. I couldn't keep my eyes open any longer.

I held Yeshua tight against me. Then lay my head down and let sleep wash over.

6

This Child

I WANTED TO do everything right.

We made sure that Yeshua was circumcised on the eighth day, and forty days after the birth we visited the temple to dedicate him to God as our first-born son and offer our sacrifice. I was determined that nothing I did would give God cause to change his mind.

Visiting the temple, and offering a sacrifice through the priests, it all felt so important to me.

It didn't take long for God to show me how wrong I was.

On the day we visited the temple, we left Beit Lechem early in the morning. We followed the road, taking the path that winds north through rocky gullies. The breeze helped as the heat increased, though by the time we cleared the ridge and got our first full view of the city, I was starting to feel tired.

Seeing the temple took my mind off this at once.

It was so impressive. Even from a distance we could make out the pillars of Solomon's colonnade and the Court of the Gentiles, and for most of the last couple of miles, Yosef and I walked in awe.

All my life I had been taught that God himself was present in the Holy of Holies, the inner part of the temple. As we approached the gleaming white stone walls that towered above us, I felt nervous and excited. I'd visited the temple each year for as long as I could remember, but this time was different.

I was a wife now, and a mother – no longer a child.

Then there was Yeshua.

Knowing that I was carrying the very baby that the prophets spoke of, and whose birth had been announced by an army of God's angels, it was at times too much even to begin to understand.

I don't know what I was expecting would happen when we finally reached the temple itself, but as we walked through the Outer Court my heart was racing faster than ever.

We bought our sacrifice from one of the priests. A pair of doves. It was the only offering we could afford – the very least that was expected for a firstborn son – but we felt proud and excited.

With our two doves ready, we stepped towards the next priest.

'This is it,' I thought. 'He's going to see Yeshua and will somehow know that this is God's chosen one.'

The priest held out his hands, took the birds, then mumbled his prayer. He didn't even look at us.

Within seconds it was over, and he had turned to the next person who was waiting behind us.

I felt confused. I looked at Yosef. *Had we got all this wrong about Yeshua?*

Yosef looked disappointed as well, but almost at once we found ourselves being hurried along with everyone else, back towards the Court of the Gentiles. It was so crowded, and I clung tight to my baby as we shuffled along.

I was so upset. I was worried too, but I was trying hard not to show it.

Then, without any warning at all, a man stepped in front of us both. He held up his hands and let out a wild cry. Like Moses parting the water, the crowd that had been pushing and shoving was held in place.

The man was old. His face was weather-beaten, but he was clearly no shepherd. He was dressed more like a merchant and he looked shrewd and wise. He had his eyes locked on Yeshua.

'Now, Lord,' he said, his voice trembling, 'you can let me die in peace, as you said!'

He reached forward and, without asking, took Yeshua from me. He held my baby up high in the air, his eyes streaming tears. I stared in disbelief. I didn't know what was happening.

'Lord, I have seen with my own eyes how you will save your people,' he said. His voice was trembling, eyes wet with emotion. 'Now all people can see your plan.' His voice trailed off. He appeared overcome and was shaking.

People were staring, but as quickly as it began, it was over. The old man handed Yeshua back to me and the crowd was moving again, flowing either side of us as if we were an island. The old man was rapidly pulled away by the crowd.

Yosef and I both stood speechless. Then suddenly we saw the old man forcing his way back towards us. His eyes were wild. Full of life and fire.

Heaving with the exertion, he shouted out once more: 'My name is Simeon, and this child is the light to reveal God to the nations . . .'

7

The Sword

SUDDENLY THE OLD man was no longer staring at Yeshua.

He was looking right at me.

He leaned in close. I could feel his breath on my face. I could see the tears in his eyes.

'This child,' he said, his voice low and quiet so that only Yosef and I could hear him, 'will be misunderstood.'

His eyes never left me.

He held out a bony finger and pointed it at my chest. 'And a sword will pierce your own heart too.'

He held his gaze for a moment, staring deep into my eyes. Then once more the crowds separated us and the old man was being dragged away.

Eventually we could see him no longer.

Yosef and I stood there, shaken and speechless, while the crowds moved around us. Slowly, we joined them and headed in the direction of the colonnade.

Nothing had gone the way I'd expected, and I just wanted to leave. But as we were walking out, another voice called out and someone else started pointing at us.

This time I knew who it was. It was the old widow who had lived in the temple for as long as I'd been visiting.

People knew her as Anna, and she was so old that her back was almost bent double. She was always sitting quietly to the side, fasting and praying. I'd never seen her talk to anyone. She was simply part of temple life. One of the many eccentrics you notice when you wander around such places.

Yet now, here she was, struggling to her feet and shuffling over towards us, shouting at the top of her voice. Her eyes were wide open, and her frail arms were shaking as she held them out to us.

I held Yeshua tight. I was a little scared of what she was going to do. But Anna didn't try to take him from me. Instead, she just started singing, in a broken voice, but so loudly.

She was praising God at full volume and people were staring – some were beginning to mock. But the words were of thanksgiving, thanking God for finally sending the child that people had been waiting for all this time.

There was so much I wanted to ask the old lady. I wanted to know how she knew about my baby – if she had also been visited by angels.

By now, Anna was attracting an unwelcome crowd around us. People were staring and whispering, pointing and jostling to get a better view.

Instinct made me hold my baby even tighter, and I knew Yosef felt uncomfortable too. He wrapped his arms around us both. As soon as we could get away, we hurried out of the temple, back into the safety of the open streets. We just wanted to go home.

We spoke non-stop on the journey back to Beit Lechem, my head so full of questions and my heart swirling with emotion. God had chosen to send Anna and the old man, Simeon, to greet our child. It felt wonderful.

Even though it had been terrifying, it had been exhilarating, and hours later, I was still shaking.

But I kept wondering why none of the priests had taken any notice of us. Why was it only a hunched, old woman and a wild-eyed man who recognised Yeshua?

If God really was sending his Son to save his people and we were right there in the temple, shouldn't some of the priests have done something? I began to doubt myself again.

And then there were the words about the sword that would one day pierce my heart. That part scared me the most.

Because I felt it was true.

8

Settling

AFTER THE VISIT to the temple that day, there were no more incidents. No more angels. No more prophecies. No more revelations.

Things settled. Months passed and life carried on as usual.

Slowly, I exhaled. Although my doubts persisted.

Yosef had decided that we would stay in Beit Lechem. I was happy to be there. Even though I missed my home, Beit Lechem was a good place for us. Yosef didn't have to work for the Romans which he hated, and we didn't have to live in a cave as we had done in Nazaret.

Plus, there were other women with children the same age as Yeshua.

If ever I needed advice or help, there were other mothers in the town I could visit. I spent as much time as I could in their company. I would sit with them while I carried out my work, listening to their stories, watching how they raised their children.

It wasn't that I had forgotten all that had happened, but these were precious days when I felt just like any other mother in Beit Lechem.

As Yeshua grew older, and he learnt to walk and started to play with the other children his age, I could spend hours happily watching him chase chickens with Ananias, his best friend, or play in the mud by the well with Joses and Yonathan, our neighbour's children.

Life in those days was simple, and I tried my best to cherish it. They were some of the best times of my life.

Even though I never thought they would last forever, I had no idea of the pain that was coming.

And I had no idea that soon, I would look back on those days and weep.

9

Three Gifts

ABOUT TWO YEARS had passed when everything changed again.

It had been an ordinary day.

It was getting dark and the first stars were coming out. I was sitting out the front with some friends, watching Yeshua and Ananias run from one side of the road to the other. I wanted him to get tired so that he might sleep through the night.

Then suddenly, I heard yelling. I looked up, worried. One of the teenagers was running towards me. Eyes wide, voice panting.

'Myriam! Strange men are looking for you! They are foreigners.'

I scooped Yeshua into my arms and hurried inside to tell Yosef. Then I heard voices outside and I knew that whoever it was had found us. I waited anxiously while Yosef went out to greet them and I tried to calm myself – and pray.

After a few minutes, Yosef invited them inside and the air was filled with scents of juniper, spices and other exotic odours I could not name. There were five of them, and I stared longer and harder than I'd ever stared at anyone in my life.

I'd never seen people dressed like them, and it was clear from their heavy embroidered cloaks and their accents that they had come from far away. To me, they looked like mystics, travellers. I was amazed at their strange appearance.

Yosef offered them water and figs, but they took little notice. They were too busy staring deep into the dark room, searching for something.

'Is the child here?' one of them asked.

Yosef tensed, but somehow I knew that I didn't need to fear them. So, I bent down and gently prized away the two little hands that had been clinging onto me behind my leg.

'It's fine,' I whispered, picking Yeshua up and holding him so that he could be seen. 'These men have come to visit you.'

As soon as they saw him, they fell to their knees. They held up their hands and started to sing in a strange voice. Little did I realise they'd spent their whole lives in preparation for this moment.

What struck me most was how they knelt, with their arms outstretched towards Yeshua. Not towards the sky. It looked so strange to me. Here they were, these men from far away, singing in this unknown language, and there was no doubting their intention: they were *worshipping* our little child.

I gently placed Yeshua down so he could stand, and the three of us just stood in shocked silence, uncertain what to do or say. I held both Yeshua and Yosef's hands tight.

And then, when they had finished bowing and praising before Yeshua – who had watched the whole thing through one eye, his little head tucked in tight against my hip – things got even more strange.

The men fumbled nervously through their satchels and brought out three intricately carved wooden boxes and laid them on the ground before us. Each box was a little bigger than my hand, and slowly the men opened each one.

In the first was a beautiful gold armlet with strange, winged creatures on each end. It was the most stunning and beautiful piece of jewellery you could imagine.

Next was some of the finest frankincense I had ever seen – the kind that is only ever used in the temple. Even wrapped in cloth and unlit, the scent drifted across the room.

And then, last of all, they opened the box to reveal a bottle no bigger than my thumb.

I looked at the man holding it. He gestured for me to take the bottle and open it.

The smell.

Instantly I was taken back home to Nazaret and the time of my grandfather's burial.

It was before the Romans raised the taxes, and so though we were poor, there was enough money to pay for a proper funeral. I was too young to help, but I had been allowed to sit in the room while the women worked.

They had bought oil to prepare the body and strips of fine linen to wrap around it, and the moment they had opened the oil, the whole room filled with a deep aroma, like sweet burning wood.

I'd sat and breathed it in slowly, and the memory has never left me.

In Beit Lechem that evening, as soon as I opened the bottle, that exact same smell filled the room. It overwhelmed me with emotion.

'Myrrh,' I said, and the men all nodded. I looked at Yosef, who was now holding Yeshua. Tighter than ever.

I knew that myrrh was a gift for burial. Our boy was two years old and yet these men had brought him something for the day that he would die.

For the first time in what seemed like a long time, fear stirred up inside me again.

10

The Warning

IT WAS TOO late for the men to travel that night, so they stayed with us, huddled in the corner of our small home that we had now made for ourselves, down the road from Yosef's cousins.

The mystic travellers seemed to sleep deeply, tired from their travels.

But me? Sleep was never going to come that night.

I'm glad that I was awake, because if I'd slept, I wouldn't have seen what happened. And if I hadn't seen it for myself, I don't think I would have had the courage to do what we did.

First, one of the men woke up. He was stressed, worried, and quickly woke the others. I couldn't understand what they were saying, but within minutes they were gathering their possessions and getting ready to leave.

I woke Yosef. He spoke to them, then quickly came back and told me that they wanted to be led to the small road that runs east.

When they all left, I was a bundle of nerves. Beit Lechem was safe enough at night, but the road east was into bandit country. I worried that Yosef might decide to accompany them beyond the town.

I lay in the dark and hoped for Yosef to return.

It took him longer than I expected, but eventually I heard his footsteps outside.

'Why did they leave like that?' I asked him as he carefully closed the door behind him.

'One of them had a strange dream. That God was warning him to go right now, and to stay away from Yerushalayim.' He started to lie back down, close into Yeshua and myself. Then he added, 'They seemed on edge. I guess they have been through a lot to have come here.'

That was all Yosef said, and he was soon asleep again. But within minutes he was stirring and breathing strangely, then he suddenly snapped back awake.

He was shaking and sweating, and I thought for a moment that he was fevered.

'It happened again, Myriam. I fear I'm going insane. It was just like before,' he said, the words tumbling out. 'Did you see him? Did he come to you too?'

'Who? What did you see?'

'The angel. I saw him again. The same one.'

A thousand questions washed over me, but before I could ask any of them Yosef was talking again.

'It was the same dream that the man had. He told it to us on the walk out of town. He had been warned about Herod, and to avoid the city. And we must go too, Myriam. It's not safe here. I feel it. The angel said that Herod is going to try to find Yeshua and kill him. We must leave here.'

My heart stopped. 'Go where?'

Yosef paused for a moment. 'Egypt. The angel said we have to go to Egypt.'

'Egypt? Why Egypt? Are you sure?'

'I am sure. And we must leave tonight. Right now.'

I didn't know what to believe. But I knew I didn't want to go. We were just beginning to feel settled in Beit Lechem. We had our small home and we had friends now. And family here. The last thing I wanted was to risk taking Yeshua out onto the roads at night. Yet I had no reason to doubt what Yosef was telling me.

Deep down, I knew that there was no other choice. If God had spoken, we needed to go.

Yosef went quickly to warn a few of his neighbours about his dream. He tried to explain everything, to ensure they remained on their guard – but that we were going to be leaving that very night.

The neighbours thanked Yosef but soon returned to their beds, saying they would discuss with the family in the morning when the others awoke. I often wonder if they thought Yosef was simply crazed. Dreams in the night are aplenty – that I know.

Meanwhile, I quickly packed our few belongings. We didn't have much, and the few gifts that the men had given us that evening were easily the most valuable things we now owned. I hid them well, knowing that without any friends or family in Egypt, we would need all we had to survive.

We prayed for our friends and hoped they would take heed of our warning. But as for us, we had to follow the instructions from the angel. It was our only assurance that Yeshua would be safe. I knew in my heart it was the right thing to do.

We crept along the quiet streets to the road that led out the west side of the town. There was good light from the moon and the stars that night, and I noticed my faint shadow behind me.

I wanted to look back. I wanted to take one last look at the place we had called home for those two years, but instead I turned my face forward, to the road ahead.

11

Murder

THE LONG DESERT journey to Egypt is still a blur to me.

My memories are jumbled, and whenever I try to remember how long we walked or what route we took, I'm stuck. All that comes to mind are endless, hot days with Yeshua on my back, and the constant fear that Herod's men were going to catch us at any time, or that bandits would set upon us.

Fear to the fleeing can be an all-consuming burden, and that fear is something I will never forget.

Herod's reputation had always been fearsome. The self-proclaimed king of the Jews, who built up the temple and constructed an apparently vast palace in the hills at Masada. Not to mention ruthless. The man who had his own wife put to death.

If we valued life and our child, we had little choice but to heed the angel and flee. For our lives, for our future.

It wasn't until we reached Egypt, across the border, that my fear started to ease. We were still far from being at peace though. We settled as best we could in a small corner of a ghetto town that was full of other people like us. One more displaced family was hardly even noticed.

What was obvious to us though, was that we were all outsiders, all on edge. So, we quietly kept ourselves to ourselves and tried to avoid attracting any sort of unnecessary attention. The reach of Herod was never to be underestimated.

Yosef and I certainly didn't have any family living this far away. And with no more visitations from angels, at times I felt so alone.

People treated us kindly, but everyone there was essentially just surviving. I quickly learnt that you can make do with just a small shelter to sleep in, work of sorts can be found, and you can visit the market like all the other women, but as a refugee it is almost impossible not to feel like an outsider.

Barely a day went by when something didn't remind me that our little family was out of place. We simply did not belong here – even in a community of friends.

But as difficult as all that was, it was nothing compared to the pain that struck several months after we arrived.

It had been an ordinary day filled with ordinary tasks. As the sun was dipping, Yosef and I visited the well. I recognised a man standing nearby. We had known him back in Beit Lechem – he was a merchant who travelled regularly between Egypt and Yehuda. I was desperate for news from home, so pointed him out to Yosef. He hurried over to talk to the man.

The sun was almost gone as I watched the conversation unfold. I was too far away to hear what they were saying, but I could tell it wasn't good news. Yosef's shoulders tensed and he looked back towards me anxiously.

I waited in silence, wondering what he could be telling Yosef. There were all kinds of possibilities, but I feared every version included the same name: Herod.

Yosef finally broke away and the merchant carried on his journey. Yosef looked ashen, in a way I'd never seen before.

'Herod's men came, as warned, to Beit Lechem,' he said quietly as we stood beside the dusty well. 'They went from house to house. Swords drawn. They dragged out all the baby boys two years old and under. When they had found them all, they gathered them all up together in the street and made them sit in a huddle.

'They had to beat the mothers and the fathers to keep them away, and any boy that tried to run was kicked back into the group.

'When they were satisfied that there were no more male children hiding in the town, they grabbed each boy in turn by the hair and slit their throats. Every single one.

'Mothers and fathers were screaming, and the blood pooled in the street. The soldiers did it in such a matter-of-fact manner, then mounted their horses and left. Not a single boy in Beit Lechem was left alive.'

My voice, when I could find it through my heaving chest, was like a stranger to me. 'Surely some escaped? You tried to warn them, Yosef. I remember.'

'Not one survived.'

I broke down on the desert ground and wept.

12

Guilt

FOR WEEKS I could think of nothing but the slaughtered.

I saw their faces in my dreams and heard their cries in the day.

Ananias. Yonathan. Joses. So many others. These were the sons of my friends. They were the boys Yeshua had taken his first steps with. The babies I had held in my own arms when their mothers needed a moment.

I felt like I too had been run through by a soldier's blade.

Yosef tried to comfort me, but nothing he said helped. I felt so much guilt. Herod had wanted to slit the throat and remove the threat of young Yeshua – but in Yeshua's absence, Herod had simply wrought terror, blood and pain to other innocents.

Doubt fell over me like a shadow.

How could any of this be in God's plan?

Months slipped by and still I felt the same way. I cannot say I wasn't fearful about the future. My little boy was still an infant, with his whole life ahead. Yet already I was dreading any more moments of pain.

I prayed I would not have to feel the sword pierce my heart like this again.

I loved my son with all my heart and soul, but I feared I would not be able to cope with the pain foretold by Simeon.

Would I be able to bear any more than the loss already, of so many children?

I asked myself this question over and over. I could find no answer.

So, I learnt to live with it. To accept that being Yeshua's mother was the greatest privilege afforded any woman, but also potentially the most painful.

Yeshua was four when we finally received news from home

about Herod. He had died. Horribly. A putrefying illness ate him from the inside.

Can any of us escape justice?

His death, though, meant that it should be a little safer for us to consider our return. Although we had heard rumour that Herod's son had since taken power – and he was reported to be crueller still.

Yet if we did not return now, then when?

Where would we return to?

'I don't care where we go,' I said to Yosef when we discussed this, late into the night. 'But I cannot return to Beit Lechem. There is too much heartache and too much risk. We must go somewhere else. Somewhere safe. Quiet.' I paused. 'We could always return to Nazaret?' I suggested tentatively.

Yosef nodded reluctantly. He had always hoped for more.

Nazaret was a poor place. It had agriculture and water, but the town was considered by many a backwater. Yet we could rebuild our lives there together.

I simply wanted to be safe. It is a mother's instinct, to protect her children and family. And I would, for as long as I was able.

The future beyond that? For Yeshua especially? That I did not know.

I knew we would be returning still to poverty, but it was the right time. I felt it.

Yosef took a deep breath. Then exhaled.

'We will go to Nazaret.'

13

The Question

SO, WE BEGAN the long, arduous desert journey, home to Nazaret in Galilee. The region we had both grown up in.

We returned to the very place where we had both seen angels. But life didn't return to the way it was when I was first pregnant, full of expectation and excitement. In many ways it went back to the way it was before all of this happened.

Yosef went back to work building houses for the Romans in Sepphoris. I returned to many of the same tasks I'd had as a younger girl – cooking, looking after little ones. I didn't mind it. Life was quiet. It was simple.

It stayed this way for years.

There were no more angels. No more visitors in the night. No need to pack up our possessions at a moment's notice and run for our lives.

I started to relax. I would trust the Lord to do his will, in his time.

In the decade that passed, there were some months when life almost felt as normal and uneventful as any other family I knew. I almost forgot that Yeshua was promised as the chosen one. The Son of God.

Almost.

Because no matter how quiet and simple our life had become, there were always the lingering questions: *Will all this quiet and simple living end? What will be the future for Yeshua? And why had all this really happened to our small, ordinary family?*

We were poor, we had lived many years as refugees, and we had little hope of any influential or prosperous future. But who was I to question God? I knew what had been told to me. So, I tried to trust that.

I asked these questions to myself a lot, but I never said them to Yosef. I didn't want to air such doubts. Life was hard enough as it was, just holding on to God's promises.

14

Lost

YESHUA WAS TWELVE and about to attend his final Passover before becoming a man. It felt like a significant time in his life, the beginning of the end of his childhood.

As we joined with others from Nazaret and made the journey down to Yerushalayim, my mind was racing. One question was shouting louder than anything else had for years: *is this the time when everything changes?*

Every time a stranger took a second look at my son, I held my breath. When we entered the temple each day, my heart was racing. I would watch Yeshua go off with the other boys his age to learn from the rabbis, half expecting to hear someone let out a cry of wonder at any moment.

But nothing happened.

The festival went along just like it always did. Everything was normal.

At the end of the three days, we joined our group of friends and family from Nazaret and began the long journey home.

There must have been fifty or sixty of us, and as usual we walked in groups, Yosef with the men, me with the women, and the children running back and forth between the two.

It was only when the light was fading, and we reached our first day's destination, that we discovered that Yeshua wasn't to be found. We raced around, asking everyone.

Nobody had seen him all day. I was starting to panic now. I started to feel sick inside.

Even though it was almost dark, I said to Yosef that I must return towards Yerushalayim straight away. But Yosef, and those around us, persuaded me that to be on the road at night would simply be a huge added danger. And not necessary.

They told me that Yeshua would be fine, and probably still

with his friends he had met in the city at Passover. He was always making new friends.

Those around me tried to make light of it, saying Yeshua would have simply forgotten we were leaving. That he was probably still playing catch with the juggling sticks that Yosef had made for him for his last birthday.

But I knew I had told him several times that we were leaving, and I was sure I had seen him when we set off all together. Well, I thought I had.

My heart was in turmoil and that night I did not sleep at all – not for one second. I felt I had let him down. And I had let God down. My job was to guard this child and bring him up. And now I had lost him.

All I could think of was Yeshua lost among the crowds. And then starting to panic and to cry. And then getting more lost.

Yosef and I were up at first light the next day, racing as fast as we could back towards the city. We kept asking anyone we met en route if they had seen our boy. Nobody knew anything.

We reached the city and carried on searching. All that day, and all that second night, we looked and knocked on doors and inns. We retraced every step, visited everywhere we could think of that Yeshua might have gone – the markets, the house we'd stayed in, the places we knew he liked, such as the outer courts of the temple.

No matter how hard we looked, we could find no trace of young Yeshua.

It was like he'd disappeared off the face of the earth.

We were feeling desperate. We kept retracing, asking everyone we saw, searching, looking, hoping. I was now sick with worry.

I kept praying and praying, for an angel to help me. Just a word. A sign. Anything to bring him back to me.

But nothing came.

Where was the angel when I needed help the most? This was the child of God. Why leave him abandoned?

I was terrified. And I just wanted my boy back.

The next morning was the worst. I was delirious with fatigue and panic by now. Yosef was also exhausted. Yet still we searched.

We had looked everywhere and were beginning to fear that he might not even be in the city at all.

Desperate, we went back to the temple for what must have been the tenth time. Instead of searching among the crowds and the traders in the outer courts, this time we pressed in to where we could see the Inner Court, where the senior rabbis taught.

And that is where we spotted him – sat among the rabbis.

Yeshua was talking, and the teachers all seemed to be listening intently.

To him.

I cried out his name and bustled past the guards, past the rabbis, right up to Yeshua and grabbed him in my arms. I couldn't stop crying.

Yeshua looked at me, surprised at my alarm, and there was an awkward silence.

'Yeshua,' I said. 'Where have you been? We've been looking for you for days.'

Yeshua blinked. He looked like he couldn't figure out for the life of him why we should be surprised by what had happened. He was almost as tall as both of us by now and he looked back and forth from Yosef to me, staring right into our eyes.

'Why did you have to look for me?'

Yosef tensed.

'Son, why did you do this to us? Your mother and I have been beyond worried for almost three days now.'

Yeshua smiled at us both and held our hands. He felt somehow different. And then I realised that he was older than sometimes we treated him.

Yeshua then gently told us, 'You should have known I must be where my Father's work is.'

I realised right then that he wasn't only my son.

Yeshua had a Father in heaven. And that, at times, his will was different to ours, his earthly parents. I smiled and continued to weep. I held him like he was a babe once again.

I would have to learn to accept that Yeshua was not mine alone.

The words of Simeon kept ringing in my ears. The sword that would one day pierce my heart.

The last few days felt like my heart had been pierced by the sword.

I could not bear to lose Yeshua ever again.

15

Saying Goodbye

I HAD BEEN so young when I fell pregnant with Yeshua. And I'm convinced that if the angel hadn't told me that Elizabeth was also pregnant with Yohanan, I would have been too paralysed by fear to do anything.

But God was good, and God was kind, and Elizabeth became my strongest support throughout the years.

It wasn't just Elizabeth and I who had the closest of friendships. Her beautiful boy Yohanan and Yeshua were like brothers. We would visit them often, and the boys would always run to meet each other. And they'd be the last to say goodbye when we had to leave.

Inseparable, spending every minute together that they could. And the mischief! It would fill a whole book.

But they were different too.

Yohanan was always the crazier of the two – and generally also the one who would come up with their escapades. Although Yeshua would need no encouragement to tag along. Always laughing, tripping over himself to keep up with Yohanan as they ran through the streets and then out into the countryside. And they'd be away for hours. One time, they were away all night too. But we were less worried this time. I knew they were together. And Yohanan had always been able to find water, food and shelter in a hundred different ways – even as a child.

The pair would invariably return filthy, covered in dust and dirt, and still laughing. They would attack the kitchen, eat enough for four men, then fall asleep on the floor.

I can see it to this day.

As they grew older, Yohanan would be the one endlessly telling stories and jokes. Yeshua was quieter, more of an observer.

I would say though, that he was the rock who gave Yohanan the confidence to shine.

Yosef always liked to riff with Yeshua and try to blame him for the troubles and scrapes the pair of them got into. And Yohanan was always happy to let Yeshua take the blame.

Those were the happiest days.

To everyone else, the pair were just like any other cousins. It was assumed that they would walk in their fathers' footsteps and learn their respective trades. It looked like Yeshua would follow Yosef and become a builder and Yohanan would become a priest.

But it didn't work out that way for Yohanan.

Yohanan didn't want to become a priest, especially as a teenager, when he started spending more and more time away from the city. He was a young man who truly hated formality, such as when Elizabeth tried to make him dress in smart clothes on Shabbat.

As he grew, he spent longer and longer periods of time on his own, out in the desert. We all knew it was where he was happiest.

Meanwhile, Yeshua's life took an unexpected turn when Yosef fell ill and died. Losing his earthly father was agony for him. I felt heart-broken for him in a way I never expected. It was as much his loss that I grieved, as my own.

Yosef had truly been a good, faithful, kind father and husband. I had been greatly blessed by having him beside me for all those difficult early years.

We wept and grieved for many months. Yeshua's sadness broke my heart.

Thankfully one of my uncles – also Yosef – was a tin merchant who lived in Arimathea. Yeshua had always been close to him, and Yosef agreed to take him on as a builder apprentice. And God knows we needed the money.

But it felt like almost overnight, Yeshua was gone. He left Nazaret, moved to Arimathea and began helping his uncle. I was happy for him. And the money provided for me. But my heart bled not to have Yeshua with me every day.

I knew the times were changing. And it was painful.

Life moved on. Years passed and there were moments when everything that had happened when Yeshua was young became a hazy memory. Yet I always knew: Yeshua's time would come.

And in time, it did.

Eighteen years, almost to the day, from when we had lost him as a boy in the temple.

It began.

16

Lamb of God

AS WITH SO many of Yeshua's earlier childhood adventures, it all started with Yohanan. Even though both men were now grown up, soon to be thirty years of age, their friendship had never waned.

Theirs was a connection that would never die.

Nobody had heard anything from Yohanan for months, but suddenly there were reports that he was on the banks of the River Yarden over near Beth 'Anya. The rumours said he was living and looking wilder than ever, dressed only in a tunic made from camel hair and a leather belt.

He walked barefoot and sustained himself on not much more than locusts and wild honey.

I smiled when I heard that part. Yohanan had always caught locusts and tried to make us eat them when he was a little boy.

But what got me were the reports of what he was doing.

People from Yerushalayim and all over Yehuda were travelling out to hear him preach. He was telling people to clean up their act and seek the kingdom of God. Maybe he would be a priest after all.

But his message was different from the religious teachers we had all listened to every week growing up. Yohanan was telling people to share their possessions with the poor; telling tax collectors to be honest; even warning Roman soldiers to stop extorting people for money.

I heard that Yohanan had even called some of the religious leaders 'snakes', and that they must change their ways.

Yohanan had always been brave.

But there was more . . .

He was specifically telling people that they needed to repent, to be baptised and to have their sins forgiven by God.

This was strange talk, far stranger than wearing camel-hair clothing or eating insects. And it was dangerous. It was the kind of thing that upset the religious elite. Because tradition said that there was only one way to the forgiveness of sins – through official sacrifices made by priests.

As we had been taught by Moses.

Whenever anyone confronted Yohanan about who he was and what he was doing, he simply replied that he was doing what was written in the ancient Scriptures:

> There is someone shouting in the desert:
> 'Prepare the way for the Lord . . . Then
> everyone will see how God will save his people!'

Some even started talking about Yohanan being the Messiah.

But Yohanan always vehemently denied it.

'I baptise with water,' he would reply, 'but among you stands one you do not know. He is the one who comes after me . . . the straps of whose sandals I am not worthy to untie.'

They were beautiful words that Yohanan would say, and to me there was no doubt: Yohanan was a true prophet, announced by an angel to Zechariah, and destined to be the one to reveal Yeshua.

Every day, the power around his message grew.

As did the crowds. People flocked to the River Yarden to see this wild man and potential prophet for themselves.

I didn't join them. Not because I didn't want to go. I longed to go to the Yarden and see him living out his calling. And I too wanted to be baptised. To be washed clean of any fears and doubts.

But deep down, I felt that this was not my time. I was to wait.

And so, I stayed at home in Nazaret and obeyed what I felt in my heart.

The waiting ended when Yeshua came to the house one day and quietly told me that he was leaving early the next day – to go and see Yohanan.

I had wondered how long it would be until Yeshua would say those words.

That evening, I packed what I needed, and before dawn I set out with Yeshua beside me.

I was strangely excited, and the journey was so beautiful. Just time with my son. I savoured every step, every moment together.

It was late in the day when we finally arrived at the river. Many of the larger crowds had thinned out, but Yohanan was still there. Still baptising. Still praying out loud and raising his hands to the heavens.

Yeshua smiled at me. Yohanan had yet to see us.

He looked even wilder than we had imagined. His clothes more like rags. His bones were poking out from his skin.

And then suddenly Yohanan saw us. His eyes were filled with pure joy, and he shouted at the top of his voice at us.

'Yeshua! Myriam!'

Yohanan started frantically wading towards us.

I couldn't help the tears as I covered my mouth from emotion and laughter.

Yohanan rushed towards us and hugged Yeshua just like they used to do when they were little, embracing and laughing together.

Yohanan turned towards the people who were standing there watching. His arm rested on Yeshua's shoulder, and in a quiet voice, Yohanan said, 'Look! The Lamb of God, who takes away the sin of the world . . .'

He paused.

'This is the one I meant when I said, "The one who comes after me . . . the straps of whose sandals I am not worthy to untie."'

The people all stared at Yeshua and waited.

'Yohanan,' said Yeshua when there was a pause. 'I want you to baptise me.'

Yohanan's face froze, mid smile. It was like he was unsure whether this was a joke he would soon be laughing at.

'Yohanan,' said Yeshua again. 'I want you to baptise me.'

Yohanan looked at me for reassurance, then back at Yeshua.

I cannot remember a time in his whole life when Yohanan was ever totally lost for words.

He held his arms out in bewilderment and looked around at those of us watching.

Then he looked back at Yeshua and spoke in the softest of voices. Such that I had rarely heard before.

'Yeshua, no. I . . . I am the one who needs to be baptised. Not you.'

Yeshua smiled and reached out and held Yohanan's hands. He wasn't going to be changed.

'Do it,' he said. 'God's work, putting things right all these centuries, is coming together right now . . .'

17

The Voice

YESHUA AND YOHANAN left me where I was, beside an old olive tree, and together, they walked towards the river.

I watched everything that followed, wiping away the tears. Tears of joy and raw emotion. I wished that Yosef could be here to witness this.

Little did I realise what was about to happen. That all of heaven was indeed watching.

I watched the two friends wade out into the water. When they were waist deep, Yohanan stopped. When he spoke, his voice was barely a whisper and I couldn't hear what he was saying to Yeshua. But I saw Yeshua nod, then Yohanan leant him back and under the water.

Yohanan held Yeshua under the water for several seconds, then he pulled him back up and Yeshua broke the surface.

At that very moment it felt as if the sky literally exploded. Everyone there could see it.

The cloud above us looked like it had simply been peeled back and parted, and the brightest sunlight I'd ever seen radiated down in a shaft onto Yeshua's head.

The normally brown waters of the Yarden sparkled, as if the surface was flecked with gold. The air suddenly tasted sweet and the whole scene was even more alive than when I'd met the angel all those years before.

Then came the voice.

It filled the sky and shook the trees. It was loud, like thunder rolling in from miles away, but so close that it seemed to me that whoever was speaking it was right beside me.

48

God himself was speaking. And that knowledge made me tremble and fall to my knees.

'You are my Son.'

The voice echoed through the sky.

I could hardly breathe with fear and excitement. And I was not alone this time – everyone on the banks around me could see and hear it too.

This was the first supernatural event I had seen with other people, and it took my breath away.

Yohanan and Yeshua were both staring up to the sky above them. Eyes wide, mouths open in rapture. Yeshua's face was glowing, his arms outstretched.

The voice continued, 'Chosen and marked by my love.'

The voice had grown louder and closer. And the wind had also suddenly picked up. Yohanan and Yeshua were still staring up above them, looking at something I could not see.

Once again, the voice spoke.

'Pride of my life.'

The strength of the voice was incredible. I could feel the power flow over me. God's love to Yeshua pouring down. It was like nothing I'd ever known.

As I looked, I finally saw what Yohanan and Yeshua were staring at. A dove. Pure white. Perfect. It was circling down towards them.

The closer it got, the brighter it became. By the time the bird was close enough to touch, the whole scene was flooded with a light that was golden like dawn.

Then the dove came to rest gently on Yeshua.

I was collapsed on the ground by now. We all were. Staring at the light and at Yeshua and Yohanan.

Then just like that, the dove took off, the light retreated and the clouds closed in. A quiet peace descended over the river.

I breathed in deeply. Still shaking.

But now I knew.

Yeshua's time had arrived.

18

The Desert

YESHUA THEN DID something extraordinary.

He waded to the far side of the River Yarden, and with the briefest of glances back at all of us gathered on the banks, he lifted his hand in a small wave, and then simply carried on walking, up towards the distant hills.

Yohanan came over to me and we stood together, silently watching as Yeshua headed away from everything he knew, owned and was.

It felt as if the seed that had been buried deep within all our lives for so many years was finally breaking the surface. And all we could do was watch.

I wasn't sure where Yeshua was even going. All I knew was that once he got beyond the hills, there was only desert.

Before long he was gone.

I stayed all the rest of the day, waiting and watching for him.

Soon it was dusk.

Yohanan suggested I travelled back to Nazaret, but I wanted to stay close to where I had watched him depart.

Even though Yeshua was now thirty years old – twice the age that I had been when I had given birth to him – the ache of motherhood felt strangely stronger than ever. He was a man for sure, and he had travelled much, but still, I could not turn my back on him, in his time of need.

As long as he was in the desert, I wanted to stay by the river and wait. I sent word to Nazaret so that no one was worried.

One of Yohanan's followers offered me a simple room in the village. I was grateful for the hospitality.

I spent the next few days sitting on the banks of the Yarden, looking towards the hills and the desert beyond. I didn't want to leave where I had been when Yeshua had been baptised and I had witnessed the heavens open.

I wanted to be here when he returned.

This place felt like my strongest connection to Yeshua – and to God. Call it a mother's intuition or just a feeling, but I sensed that there was something important he had to do out there. Alone.

I just prayed he would return soon.

When we had lost him that time in the temple as a twelve-year-old boy, I felt a similar sense of trepidation. The words he spoke when we had finally found him came back to me, again and again: 'You should have known I must be where my Father's work is.'

I was convinced that the same thing was happening now.

The desert was right where his Father wanted him.

Meanwhile, at the River Yarden, Yohanan continued to attract fresh crowds. Each day, they grew ever bigger, as people started hearing about what had happened at the river.

I enjoyed listening to his teaching and watching him baptise so many. Elizabeth had left us all heart-broken when she died some years before, and I hoped that it was comforting to Yohanan to have me there, smiling from beneath a shaded tree.

At first, I didn't mind the waiting. I liked it. It was calm and quiet among the olive trees, and I did a lot of thinking.

I thought about why Yeshua had chosen to cross the River Yarden and head into the desert. It reminded me of Moses leading the Israelites through the desert for forty years.

I let myself imagine what it must have been like then, to see Moses lead his people out of the wilderness and into their new homeland. How the moment they crossed the Yarden marked the end of their slavery and the beginning of their new life that God himself had promised.

After almost a week had passed with no sign of Yeshua, I started to worry. I kept thinking how he had said nothing to any of us, about where he was going, or why, or how long he would be away for.

He had taken no food and barely any water with him.

You can't last long in the desert in such heat with no supplies or tools or shelter. I knew that much.

So I did what I do best – I prayed. All day. For my son.

Yet once again, Yeshua did not return.

I soon felt maybe I should go home to Nazaret. I told Yohanan to send word to me if anyone saw Yeshua. I promised to return to the River Yarden every Shabbat, and to keep waiting and praying.

But as one week turned to two, then two to three, I still heard no news from Yohanan. And each time I returned to the Yarden, there was still no sign of Yeshua.

How much longer would he be? How much longer could he be? I had a bitter feeling that something was wrong, that Yeshua was in trouble.

There were days when I wanted to get up and go to the desert myself, to try to find him. To help him. *As if an old woman like me could be of use to God's own Son.*

That thought was futile. There was nothing I could do for Yeshua.

The thought was another stab in my heart.

When God's voice had filled the sky at Yeshua's baptism, it marked the beginning of his true journey – and the end of mine.

I would always be his mother, but he ultimately belonged to his Father in heaven.

It wasn't easy to accept this.

19

Human Limits

TWENTY-FIVE DAYS AFTER Yeshua had left, still none of us had heard any news.

I went every week to the River Yarden, as promised, and waited. Watching. But there was no sign.

It was the same at thirty-five days.

Every day, my fear grew bigger.

There was a physical limit to how long a human could survive in such desert extremes. And I felt we were close to that time.

But how could this be God's plan? Surely, God would not allow his only Son to die?

It took forty days before Yeshua returned. When he finally reappeared, it was my fifth trip back to the river. I had never lost hope. And I had never stopped praying.

At first, Yeshua was just a speck on the horizon. A shadow moving slowly among the rocks. But I knew it was him. I could feel him.

I stood up and followed his every step.

He was only managing a few paces at a time. The closer he got, the more I could see how much he was struggling. His clothes hung off him. He looked even more wild and ragged than Yohanan. He looked broken.

I called out to him, and ran to go towards him. But he slowly waved a hand back to me, telling me to stay where I was.

I stood and watched as he shuffled down to the far bank of the Yarden, threw his head in to drink for the longest time, then waded across.

Over the years, I'd seen him come back from many trips into the desert. But never for so long and never alone.

And I'd never seen him look anything close to this.

He waded out of the water near to where I was.

The Yarden had washed away some of the dust, but still his skin was burned and sore. He had cuts and scabs all over his hands, and his feet were raw in places where his sandals had once been.

He was stick thin. He had grown a patchy beard and he smelled like he had been living among wild animals for the whole forty days that he had been in the desert.

He was mumbling as he shuffled towards me, and the closer he got, the more I could hear. He was repeating a mantra to himself: *Man cannot live on bread alone, but on every word that comes from the mouth of God.*

When he finally stood before me, I could instantly see that something had changed in him. It was his eyes.

They were wild. Yet also clearer, more determined than I'd ever seen them.

I'd known that he was ready, from the moment he had been baptised.

Now, looking at his eyes, I could see that he knew it too.

20

Come with Me

AS YESHUA RECOVERED his strength, I was determined to stay near him for as long as possible.

Every day, I was there. Fussing over him, soothing and caring for his wounds, feeding him dates, raw honey, milk and any meat we could spare. He ate and got stronger.

Soon he was laughing with us all and recounting stories of his survival in the desert, with no food and all alone. The stories were often against himself, and he always laughed the hardest. Then he would eat some more.

I kept reminding him to take it slow, but he barely listened. I knew though, that forty days without food had put an incredible strain on his body. And his mind. Yet as he recovered physically, I noticed too that he was more focused than I had ever known him.

Clear headed. Ready.

And soon, Yeshua didn't want to rest any longer among the family. He wanted to be out.

He would spend his days talking with many groups of different people. As soon as Yohanan had told his followers, 'This is the one I was talking about! This is God's chosen one,' that moment changed things.

People started to seek Yeshua out. Wherever he went.

Strangers would literally follow him, like they had known him their whole lives.

I first noticed the effects of this change over Yeshua one evening, when he was returning to a village we were visiting. Two men raced up alongside behind him.

'What do you want?' Yeshua asked gently.

They were nervous. Just staring at him. Like he was from some other world. It made me smile.

'Rabbi,' one of them said, his voice shaky. 'Where are you staying?'

Yeshua looked at them both, then smiled.

'Come with me,' he said.

He led them back to the small place we were staying for the night. The three of them sat down together, and while I organised food and drink for us all, they listened to Yeshua.

He told them to love the poor; serve their neighbour. He told them how to be truly forgiven and how to be free – and everyone listened in awe.

I had heard Yeshua say such things before – he often spoke of freedom – but never in the same way that he was speaking now. He somehow appeared to have more authority. He spoke with a fervent intensity and a gentle power.

When he opened his mouth, he didn't just speak words, he taught.

To those who listened, he revealed the world, themselves and others, in a way they had never seen before.

21

The Wedding

EVEN THOUGH WE didn't know the bride's family very well, I had promised them we would be there. After all, weddings are always such wonderful times of celebration, and the invitation was a kindness to our family that I didn't want to refuse.

I had asked Yeshua to come with us, but I was worried he might forget. He was so consumed by people nowadays, and he was away from the region for longer and longer periods.

It seemed wherever he went, more crowds followed.

I longed for the lazy days in Nazaret, when Yeshua was younger. No pressures, no places to be, people to see. Where had those times gone?

It didn't take long for our family to reach Kana, and we were all soon swept up in the busyness of the celebrations. I'd sent word on to Yeshua to remind him that he was invited, but still I didn't know whether he was actually going to attend.

The day of the wedding, the ceremony had been completed, and I'd almost resigned myself to Yeshua not coming. Then midway through the early evening festivities, he showed up.

He was not alone. He had four men with him. I recognised two as those who had followed him to where we had been staying that time. Yeshua introduced them to me as two brothers, Shimon and Andreas.

The guests were all talking and laughing, and many of the village children were still running around playing. Soon it would be their bedtime.

Hardly anyone here took much notice of Yeshua and his friends. If they did recognise him, it was more likely to be as just Yeshua, the builder from Nazaret. Small regions are like that.

More and more, Yeshua seemed to enjoy these brief moments of normality. When he could just be among friends and family. He could stop and enjoy their company, no one wanting anything from him. He could relax a little.

The evening continued, the sun disappeared and fires were lit. The music, wine and laughter was flowing freely. Soon everyone was dancing under the stars.

I was so happy Yeshua had made it. I spotted him laughing with some old friends. Like old days.

The whole atmosphere was pure celebration.

I am too old for much dancing, so after a while I went to the side. I sat with the widows and smiled and watched the young making fools of themselves.

It was because I was sitting down, away from the main party that I noticed the problem. The servers were all whispering among themselves, and they looked stressed. I leant over to one of them and gently asked if I could help at all.

She thanked me and said that all was fine. But it was clear it wasn't.

Then I spoke to the head server. 'Please let me help,' I told him.

As soon as the head server told me the issue, I relaxed. It really wasn't a disaster. The wine had all but run out. It was a shame for the party, but not the end of the world.

Yet just then, I felt my heart beat a little faster, and a thought came into my head.

Yeshua could help.

I quickly went and found him. He was sweaty, and Andreas and Shimon were laughing with him as they all danced.

I called to him. 'Yeshua, come here for a moment.'

He reluctantly came to me, and I gently pulled his cloak, leading him towards the serving area so we could talk.

'Yeshua,' I paused. 'They're almost out of wine.'

Yeshua looked at me, a big grin on his face. Still out of breath from dancing. He was about to brush it off and return to the dancing when he looked at the three servers staring nervously back at him.

Finally, he looked back at me. His smile was gone.

'Is this any of our business?' he said, his voice low.

I gave him a look only a mother can give. 'They need some help, Yeshua.'

I held his gaze and squeezed his hand.

'This isn't my time,' he replied as he started to pull away.

I didn't say a word. I just looked at him. And held onto his hand. I wasn't letting go.

'Don't push me,' Yeshua added more seriously.

The silence between us was strong, but I felt it was right to push him – just a little. A gentle nudge to open those wings and fly. Only a mother can know that time.

I gave him one last smile then turned to the servers.

'Whatever he tells you to do, just do it.'

I turned and moved away from Yeshua and the servers. And I watched.

Yeshua had his gaze fixed on the large jars – and a strange silence descended. He stood there, suddenly very still. As if lost in his thoughts: *'Was it time?'*

Yeshua hesitated for a few moments longer.

Then he turned to the servers, and nodding, he gently told them, 'Fill the jars with water.'

He was pointing at the six huge stone water vessels. Each could contain about 25 gallons of water.

The servers looked surprised, and then looked at each other, as if thinking: *'What? All of them? That's a lot of water!'*

I could see their hesitation. 'Do as he says,' I encouraged.

The servers moved quickly. They worked together and started to load up the huge jars with almost 150 gallons of water from the well.

When they were finished, Yeshua told them to fill their pitchers from the jars and go and serve the host and guests.

The servers looked worried now. The host was a good man, but he wouldn't be happy if they tried to trick him, and his guests, by pretending plain old water was wine.

Again, I encouraged them on. To obey Yeshua. So, they did. And soon they started to pour from the pitchers into the empty cups of the guests, and host.

I had wanted so badly to look in the water jars for myself,

to see if anything had happened, but I resisted. Instead, I just stayed beside my son, and watched.

Just then, some of the first servers came rushing back to us, the blood drained from their faces. They looked shell shocked. Then the words came tumbling out.

'It's incredible!' one said, hardly able to breathe with excitement.

'They say it's the best wine they have ever tasted.'

Then another of the servers chipped in, 'Look! Taste it! Taste it for yourself . . .'

PART TWO

Ta'om, Sceptic

KANA
C. AD 29

Small village in the hills above Galilee, overlooking the Roman town of Sepphoris. Known for its vineyards, Synagogue and independence fighters.

22

Water into Wine

I'D BEEN WATCHING him carefully.

As soon as I noticed the servers panicking, I saw Myriam take Yeshua over to speak with them. That made me curious. I wanted to see what all the fuss was about.

I couldn't hear what his mother was saying to him, but she was doing all the talking. He was standing there, teasing her, trying to get her to dance. But it was obvious that she wanted him to do something – and she wasn't taking no for an answer.

It seemed Yeshua finally relented.

I couldn't see exactly what was going on with the stone jars, but I could see the change in the servers' faces when they saw what they were pouring out. The moment they realised what Yeshua had done, they looked like they'd seen a ghost.

The guests were going wild. Toasting the host and praising the party.

I've been to a lot of wedding feasts and seen a lot of people drink too much and get way too overexcited, but this was different. Everyone and everything went crazy – the dancing, the laughter, and ever more cheers for the host who had apparently surprised and delighted them all.

To be honest, I didn't really know what all the fuss was about. I thought that everyone was just getting a bit carried away. Somebody had found some decent wine, that was all. Maybe Yeshua had found some out the back.

But a few things didn't quite make sense.

Then one of the servers came up to me and put a cup in my hand. She was giggling. It seemed the servers were also now included at the party. That part I did notice.

The server filled my cup until it was almost overflowing and then stood smiling, waiting for me to take a drink. Inquisitively, I took a gulp.

Oh, that taste!

I couldn't describe it then, and I can't find the words now. Like a taste of heaven – if back then I even believed heaven existed. I finished the cup and let out a sigh. Then I shook my head in amazement.

I needed to speak to Yeshua – now.

What had he done to that water? I'd watched them fill the pitchers from the well.

How was it now somehow turned into wine?

It's one thing pulling out a nice bottle from under your hat, it's another turning 150 gallons of well water instantly into the most exquisite tasting wine any person at the gathering had ever drunk.

It wasn't just odd; it was outrageous. And it needed explaining.

But try as I might, I couldn't get Yeshua away from all the dancing and singing. This party was in full swing.

Then one of the burly fishermen yelled at me, arms aloft. 'We're going to Yerushalayim soon.' He then stumbled towards me. 'You should join us.' He wasn't the first fisherman I'd seen having had too much to drink.

I shrugged him off and stood there. Confused.

'And no, I'm not going to Yerushalayim,' I thought to myself.

I never act rashly. I don't do spontaneous. I like well-thought-out plans that have solid foundations. But something that evening changed in me. Something made me even more curious about Yeshua.

I wanted to make up my own mind about whether he was for real or not. Or whether he was simply some magician who had figured out how to turn water pitchers into prime wine.

Whether it was this curiosity, or that one cup of wine, I suddenly found myself saying to the fisherman, 'Yes, I'll join you.'

And that's how it started.

23

Turning Tables

YESHUA AND HIS family returned to Kfar Nahum for a few days, and I then caught up with the group on their way south. Their numbers had grown a little.

Some of us with him were new, like me. Others, like Shimon, Andreas, Yakov and a different man called Yohanan, had been hanging around with him for longer.

They were simple fishermen and traders from Galilee but there seemed to be a special bond between them all and Yeshua.

They were tight.

As for me, I was content to be an observer.

It had been a while since I had been to Yerushalayim for Passover. I've never liked the city much – all those crowds. And the closer we got, the more uncomfortable I felt. Especially when we saw the Roman troops.

The other followers all had their eyes locked on Yeshua, but I couldn't take my eyes off all those Roman centurions marching down from their garrison further up the coast. We must have seen hundreds, probably thousands of them, all marching in tight formation along the trade roads.

They'd strut along the roads with their weapons and their disdain for us on display. They'd take up all the space and force the rest of us to step aside and make way. I considered them like vermin.

The atmosphere was always tense near soldiers. People in the region lived with fear every day. The Roman message to every Jew they passed was always clear: comply or there will be violence.

By the time we finally arrived at the city and reached the temple, I wasn't thinking so much about Yeshua, but about the Romans. How tragic it all was to be celebrating Passover

– the moment God rescued our ancestors from slavery to the oppressive Pharaoh of Egypt – while the Roman troops ruled over us with an iron fist.

Had anything really changed at all?

We were just living in the past, pretending that we were free, when we were as trapped as ever. We'd traded one master for another.

As we joined with the crowds beneath the Pool of Siloam and climbed up towards the temple's southern entrance, I felt a little disappointed with Yeshua. Everyone around him was singing psalms of supposed victory.

This sense of hope that seemed to be growing among everyone felt misplaced, almost pathetic.

Hope is dangerous to the powerless.

The wine was one thing, and maybe I couldn't quite figure that out yet, but I couldn't fight the feeling that Yeshua was just another good man, hopelessly doing his best. Yet ultimately, cruelly spreading false hope.

One party trick wouldn't change that feeling.

There was no simple solution for our people, not while the Romans ruled our land.

I fell back behind the others, away from him and the rest of his group of friends. I was hot, away from home and beginning to think that I'd maybe made a mistake coming even this far.

I was lost in my thoughts when I heard raised voices up ahead. It sounded like Yeshua was shouting at someone. I'd never heard him raise his voice. That got my attention.

I pressed through the crowd, into the outer courts of the temple. When I got there the shouting was over, but something serious had happened. There were tables flipped over, and some of the money traders were scrambling around on the floor, picking up their coins. There were a whole lot of angry people shouting at Yeshua.

And as for him, he looked enraged.

He was holding a whip made from strands of leather bound together, and his knuckles were white from gripping it so hard.

'Show us a sign from God,' yelled one of the traders angrily at Yeshua. 'Prove that you have the right to do these things.' The trader paused. 'Because you don't!'

Yeshua's eyes flashed as his voice simmered with emotion. Then he slowly raised his voice so all could hear him and exclaimed, 'Destroy this temple and I will rebuild it in three days.'

That instantly set them off, arguing about how it had taken decades to construct, and then they all started bustling around, picking items up and righting tables. Others shouted more abuse back at Yeshua from a distance.

I didn't care what they were all arguing about. I just couldn't take my eyes off Yeshua.

He was standing there, his eyes still full of fire. The whip twitching in his hand.

He looked primed to fight anyone who came close to him.

People kept their distance.

Yeshua looked dangerous.

But there was something about him I couldn't quite pin down.

He wasn't like all the other teachers. He didn't want to play the same old games and keep pretending that life was just as it was meant to be. That our old rituals would somehow suffice.

It was as if everyone just wanted us to stay compliant. To keep the status quo.

But Yeshua appeared to be preparing to go further.

Much further.

If you cause chaos in the temple in Yerushalayim, you're asking for trouble. Not just from the Romans but from the Jewish spiritual leaders. Both were dangerous.

To me, his intensity and anger showed the spirit of a renegade. But strangely I liked it.

Maybe Yeshua really did want to take on the system? And even fix it? God only knew.

As for destroying and rebuilding the temple, well, to me the whole rotten system was broken and needed rebuilding anyway.

And as for the three days part? I liked Yeshua's style. He had made me take notice.

Just like the first gulp of wine back in Kana, the whole experience lasted only a moment. But all these moments were changing me. Inside. And for now, that was intriguing.

I wasn't sure where all this was going. But I decided to stick around.

24

Reborn

WHAT YESHUA DID in the temple that afternoon focused all our attention, and we were still talking about it late into the night, gathered in a house on the outskirts of the city.

I was nervous though of what the repercussions would be for us all.

Hanging around with Yeshua was suddenly taking on a whole new level of risk.

You don't do that sort of thing in the temple, walk out and that's the end of it. I knew his actions would create a hornet's nest.

All our talking stopped the moment someone knocked on the door, asking to meet with Yeshua.

The man was wearing a cloak and was keeping the hood low over his face. When he was inside, he pulled it off cautiously and introduced himself as Nicodemus. I'd heard the name before and was vaguely aware that he was a Pharisee and teacher of the law – a man of significant importance.

Devout, and dedicated to upholding and adhering to the religious law.

It didn't take long before the whispers went around the group that he wasn't just any teacher, but a member of the Sanhedrin.

That meant important. And powerful.

This worried me even further.

A lot of our group also now looked nervous, but Yeshua appeared to take it all in his stride. He invited Nicodemus to sit and talk.

What can I say about the conversation that followed?

Yeshua started by talking about rebirth.

'I'm telling you,' he said, looking straight at Nicodemus, 'no one can see the kingdom of God unless they are born again.'

Nicodemus, the great religious teacher, looked confused. He stumbled around for words.

'How can anyone,' he stammered, a nervous smile flickering on his face, 'be born again, who has already been born and grown up?' He paused. 'You can't re-enter your mother's womb . . .'

Yeshua's face was intense. Then he broke out into a warm smile, and everyone relaxed with him.

All this talk was tiring. And confusing to many of us. Including Nicodemus.

As for the fishermen, their willingness to keep up with all this chat had long gone, that much I could decipher.

But Yeshua persevered with Nicodemus.

'When you look at a baby,' Yeshua explained, 'it's just that: a body you can look at and touch. But the person who takes shape within is formed by something you can't see and touch – the Spirit – and becomes a living spirit.' He paused. 'So don't be so surprised when I tell you that you have to be "born from above" – out of this world, so to speak.'

That night, Yeshua spoke of so many things, and Nicodemus listened. Like a baby drinking in its mother's milk, he absorbed it all. His face was deeply furrowed as the words of Yeshua rained down upon him.

Yeshua told him that it was necessary for the Son of Man to be lifted up. Nicodemus pressed him further.

What did he mean?

'The Son of Man must be lifted up – that everyone who believes may have eternal life in him.'

He paused, considering every word.

'God did not send his Son into the world to condemn the world, but to save the world, through him.'

Yeshua let the words hang. Then he explained further.

'For God so loved the world that he gave his one and only Son, that whoever believes in him shall not perish but have eternal life.'

The words dripped like honey off a hive. And they poured right into my heart. And the heart of Nicodemus.

It was the first time any of us had heard such words of life. Words of life for us all.

Was Yeshua saying he had come to save the entire world?
Who was he claiming to be?

Part of me tried to resist Yeshua. To stop myself daring to believe. But when I was with him, I felt like I was in the presence of pure goodness.

And I had never felt that before.

And what about claiming to be the 'Son of Man'?

I noticed Yeshua often called himself this. And how uncomfortable it made many of the Pharisees. The implication was always clear: it was claiming authority from heaven above.

That night, long after Nicodemus had pulled his cloak up over his head and slipped out into the darkness, I sat alone and thought.

With Yeshua, everything was upside down. He turned water into wine. He took a whip to the people who strutted around the temple, brimming with self-importance. Yet he called everyday people, like fishermen, even sceptics like me, his closest friends.

He was, in turn, spectacularly normal, then somehow totally of another world.

He was unlike anyone I had ever even imagined. And I couldn't help my heart beginning to trust what he was telling us.

Little did I know that soon it would be my turn to be confused by Yeshua. And when he turned my world view upside down, I wasn't so sure I liked it.

25

Enemy Territory

I WAS SURPRISED when I heard we were going to be heading north through Samaria. But after the night with Nicodemus, Yeshua told us that we were going back to Galilee by the most direct route, straight into the heart of that godforsaken region.

I considered the plan madness.

All my life, I'd avoided that place. It wasn't just the danger – after all, danger was everywhere with the Romans. But Samaria was in a class of its own in terms of low-life, low morals, and as far as any Jewish person was concerned, it was number one on the unclean places to avoid.

You could call it enemy territory – especially if you wanted to keep your reputation and credibility intact. And for Yeshua, who was now speaking to more and more people of influence, you might think reputation and credibility would be important.

As far as I was concerned, I thought Yeshua was mad to want to go right through the heart of that troubled place.

We headed out of the city and stayed one night in Beth 'Anya, at the home of Yeshua's friend, Elazar, and his sisters, Marta and Myriam. It would be the last bit of light-hearted downtime before we set off.

As we got closer to Samaria, the quieter and more anxious we all became. For once, there was little chatter among us. By the time we finally crossed into the land of the people who had been our enemies for generations, we were walking in silence.

I remember hearing how a band of Samaritans had once defiled the temple in Yerushalayim by scattering the bones of dead people in the inner sanctuary. The ultimate desecration.

People don't forget that sort of cultural and religious abomination.

Yeshua, though, looked like he was having the time of his life. That worried me even more.

What did he know that we didn't?

In Samaria, there were none of those wide, fast Roman roads we were used to. Instead, Yeshua led us through narrow mountain passes, along steep ravines and twisting goat tracks. Somehow, he knew exactly where he was going, and he kept a brisk pace, barely stopping at all.

I didn't mind the haste. As far as I was concerned, the sooner our time in Samaria was over, the better.

We slept where we stopped, off the track and in the hills. It wasn't glamorous living, on the dust, round a small fire, with limited food and water. But we were glad to be together at least.

Two days after we'd left Yerushalayim, we were walking down a narrow valley that runs between Mount Ebal and Mount Gerizim. We needed supplies, so we dropped down to a small town called Sychar. We still had a day of walking ahead of us before we were out of Samaria.

It was the hottest part of the day, and I was hoping that we'd just buy some food, refill water, then press on. Samarian outback villages aren't good places to hang about.

On the outskirts of Sychar, Yeshua peeled off the main track and started to head towards the well. The others wanted to go directly to the village to get supplies, so I quickly collected their water skins and followed at a little distance behind Yeshua.

A lone woman was already at the well drawing a bucket up, and as Yeshua approached, I saw her stop, spy him and look him over suspiciously.

I don't know how to say it, but to me, she looked like trouble — not the sort you'd find in the city temple – let's put it like that.

She had the appearance of everything that I felt summed up this region. Rough – and on the make.

I didn't trust the look of her one inch.

And I wasn't going to get any closer.

So, I sat down behind a rock and just watched.

26

Well Water

GOD ONLY KNOWS what Nicodemus would think if he could see Yeshua with this woman now.

The thought made me chuckle.

I was also certain that Nicodemus' Sanhedrin brethren would not be here either.

Not in Samaria, not near this woman.

The fact that she was at the well during the hottest part of the day was another warning. You collect water when it's cooler, and you do it with others. Hauling buckets is hard work.

But this woman went to get her water when everyone else was not.

That confirmed what I had already felt when I first spied her. She was trouble. And in Samaria, when there is trouble, you can double it.

This will be interesting, I thought as I watched Yeshua approach her.

Part of me wanted to warn him to be careful of this type of woman, but then part of me was also intrigued, as to how Yeshua would handle this.

Then I saw him start to talk to her.

'Please give me a drink,' he gently asked her.

The woman replied with a tone of flirtatious sarcasm. 'I'm surprised you ask me for a drink,' she paused. 'You being a Jew and me a Samaritan.' She flicked her hair at him as she carried on pulling up her water bucket.

'You don't know what God can give you,' Yeshua replied. 'And you don't know who I am.'

The woman stopped and turned to him.

Her look said it all: *Go ahead, enlighten me, oh rabbi.*

She was dripping attitude as well as water, as she started to decant the bucket into her clay jar.

Yeshua continued. 'If you knew, you would have asked me, and I would have given you living water.'

The woman stopped once more. A smile broke across her face. She suddenly seemed to be enjoying this.

'And from where will you get this living water?' she laughed. 'The well is deep and you have nothing to get it with.' She wasn't going to be played by some itinerant rabbi. 'Are you greater than our ancestor Jacob? The one who gave us this well.'

She looked like she had put Yeshua firmly in his place, as she turned to leave.

But Yeshua reposted on a different tack.

'Go get your husband and come back.'

The woman turned back with a sarcastic smile. 'I have no husband.'

'You are right,' Yeshua instantly replied. 'You have had five husbands, and the man you live with now is not your husband.'

The woman stopped in her tracks. Her tightly clasped hands put down the water bucket and she turned, staring at Yeshua.

She looked suddenly frightened and stuttered out the words. 'I can see you're a prophet.' She was moving away now from Yeshua. As if this man before her was some sort of sorcerer – or worse.

She couldn't help talking. 'And I know the Messiah is coming.' It was all she could manage to say, hoping it would appease this strange man before her.

Yeshua held his look. It was a look of such love and kindness that it took me off-guard.

The woman looked unsure of what was happening. Her cheeks were raw with emotion. She repeated herself nervously. 'I know the Messiah is coming.'

Yeshua then nodded.

'He is talking to you now. I am the Messiah.'

27

The One?

IT WAS AT that moment that the others came into view, approaching the well.

They looked at Yeshua and this Samaritan woman, who now looked plainly terrified.

When she spotted the others, she turned and ran back towards the village, leaving the bucket of water still half-decanted on the ground.

I wasn't sure what to say to everyone when they asked what had been happening. So, I chose to say nothing.

Yeshua knew though.

We started a small fire nearby in the shade, to cook something to eat. But I didn't feel like food now, even though an hour earlier I had been ravenous.

Yeshua smiled at me warmly, then sat there looking across the Samarian valley.

Had I heard him correctly? The Messiah?

A cloud of fog was swirling around my head.

I tried to focus. Things were getting much stranger now – in my head, my heart and on the ground. I needed time to process this.

I knew that Yeshua was a good man, of that I had no doubt. And I also knew he had a dangerous side. He didn't seem to care much about offending some people or kicking over a few money lenders' carts. Not to mention kicking over some egos.

Yet, then there were moments such as with this woman . . . His gentleness, his seemingly miraculous insights, not to mention his sense of fun.

He was incredible to be around.

But when it came to claiming to be the Messiah, the Saviour of the world . . . that was taking it to another level.

To me, those weren't the sort of words that a so-called good man went around saying. A mad man maybe.

Could Yeshua not simply be a prophet? After all, they say Yohanan the Baptiser was a prophet.

But I knew enough to understand that prophets were inspired teachers who told us *about* God. They didn't go around acting as if they had all the authority *of* God. Claiming to be the actual Messiah.

What about the fact that so many had witnessed Yohanan clearly proclaim Yeshua to be the Lamb of God who would take away the sins of the world?

And if he was the Messiah, then why not save us from these Romans?

Instead, he seemed to spend a lot of time attacking the sacred temple and hanging out with the culturally unclean, promising them water of life.

It was all confusing.

A mystery.

And right now, I could find no satisfactory answers.

As I was lost in these thoughts, I noticed the woman from earlier returning to the well – but this time she was not alone. A crowd was with her, and it was obvious that they didn't like her much.

She was out front, pointing towards us, and they were all holding back behind her. They looked suspicious.

This time though, as she rushed towards Yeshua, she cried out and fell at his feet. I could hardly gather what she was saying, her words were drowned out by her tears.

We all just stared awkwardly.

Now, of course, I look back and wonder why we were so surprised. Before long, this sort of response would happen all the time. And often with the most unlikely of people.

Endless needs being met, endless intrigue piqued, endless love and mercy shown.

But that first time in Sychar, at that well, it was all very new, and very confusing.

And I suppose at heart, I was still sceptical that a man could also somehow be God.

How was it possible?

What I did know was that if I were the Messiah, come to reveal myself on earth, I'm not sure an outcast, Samaritan woman would be the best or most reliable person to announce the news to.

But then again, who was I to judge?

Yeshua always did things in his own beautiful way.

We ended up staying in that Samarian village for two days. That was something else I would never have predicted. And that they were such good people.

I watched and listened as Yeshua spent time with them – talking, laughing, teaching. All day and all evening.

As we departed on the third morning, one of the Samaritan village leaders came up to me and said, 'He really is the one who will save the world.'

28

My Shame

I COULD FEEL this change happening within me. And it was raw and uncomfortable. Yeshua was turning a lot of my long-held ideals on their head. And I wasn't at all sure what to make of it.

It was to the downtrodden and the mistrusted that he chose to reveal his identity. That was intriguing.

It was to that outcast, Samaritan woman that he would entrust this revelation.

Not us. Not me.

Maybe I was the one who needed to re-examine my reflection in the well water.

That moment with the woman had been beautiful to observe, but also painful for me to experience. A realisation that she was not the unclean one to be avoided. I was.

I was ashamed and embarrassed by my judgements of her – ashamed of so much prejudice I knew I held in my heart. I was embarrassed to let Yeshua see just how far from his own loving, inclusive, affirming nature I really was.

Everything he did seemed to be a revelation, an example, a chance to make things complete, healed and whole.

Whether he was who he said he was, I wasn't yet sure.

Time would tell – but I committed to stay with him a little longer.

29

Word Spreads

THE MOMENT WE heard that Yohanan the Baptiser, Yeshua's cousin, had been put in prison by Antipas, the son of Herod, something significant changed.

I never really knew Yohanan. But I knew how close the cousins were.

Before Yohanan's arrest, Yeshua almost always kept a low profile, his temple outburst being an exception.

Even his own mother had been the one to persuade him to act at the wedding, and the meeting with Nicodemus had been completely private.

Even his encounter with the woman in Sychar, even though it had been a clear indication of who he claimed to be, the moment took place in Samaria, so few were ever going to take that seriously.

But after Yohanan was imprisoned, for speaking out against Antipas' infidelities, that was the moment when something shifted in Yeshua. From then on, he was all in. Non-stop. Tell the world and show the world. There was no more hiding, no more wondering about whether the time was right.

And what he did next would be sure to get Antipas' attention – the very man who had arrested Yohanan the Baptiser.

We were back in Kana one day, the place where Yeshua had turned those jars of water into fine wine, when suddenly one of the King's officials came running up to Yeshua. He had heard news that he was in town.

The King's official then humbly knelt before Yeshua.

This got my attention. There are not many times you see royal officials kneeling at the feet of a poor builder-turned-travelling teacher from Nazaret. But then again, I had got used to the unexpected with Yeshua.

The royal official begged him to come at once to his home, saying his son was dying. I admired his courage and faith in Yeshua, especially with the crowds watching on. But the official looked desperate.

I was intrigued how Yeshua would respond. But he simply turned and started walking away. I could see a mix of fatigue and exasperation on his face. Then Yeshua spoke back to the official, and to all the people of Kana listening: 'Unless you people are dazzled by a miracle, you refuse to believe.'

But the official simply ignored the rebuke and kept pleading for his help. 'Come,' he begged. 'It's life or death for my son.'

Yeshua paused, but this time there was no dismissal. No turning and walking away. There was just a look – the same look I'd seen in Samaria, when it seemed as though Yeshua was holding the pain, fear and sorrow of this broken world on his own shoulders.

Then Yeshua leaned in close, dropped his head and smiled. He placed a hand on the man's shoulder. 'Go home,' he said. 'Your son lives.'

The official didn't wait a beat.

He turned and ran, leaving us standing there, surrounded by a few curious onlookers. Gradually they disappeared too, leaving Yeshua and us to ourselves once more.

We decided to stay nearby, and we spent the rest of the day eating and relaxing.

It was one of the last times that it was easy for us to be alone together.

Two days later, we were still in Kana, buying breakfast at the market. Yeshua had gone off to be alone in the hills, which he often did, especially first thing in the mornings.

Suddenly, I spotted a man hurrying towards us. He was rich, and clearly not used to rushing around after people. He was drenched in sweat, out of breath and talking in a hushed tone.

'Is it true? Are you one of his followers?'

'Why? What's happened?' I asked.

'The rabbi you're with. Yeshua. Did he really tell the official that his son would live? Did you see them talking?'

'I did. I heard their conversation with my own ears.'

'And when did he say it? Was it sometime around the seventh hour?'

'I don't know for sure, but yes, probably sometime just after midday.'

'Astounding,' said the man, mopping the sweat from his face. 'The boy is my nephew, and I was there all morning while my brother came to find your Yeshua. We all feared the boy would be dead by nightfall. It was not looking good at all.'

He paused.

'But then, without warning, right around the seventh hour, the boy just suddenly sat up, perfectly healthy. Like nothing had ever happened.'

The man shook his head as he recounted the story. 'Quite remarkable,' he added. 'Remarkable.'

We talked for a little longer, then I watched as the man scurried around the market, telling anyone and everyone who would listen what had happened.

The news spread like fire.

When Yeshua came back to the village an hour later, we were still in the market centre. As he wandered over towards us, every face turned to look at him. The place went silent.

Without any introduction or explanation, Yeshua started speaking to everyone in a loud voice, with authority:

'The time has come!'

Nobody moved. Nobody spoke.

'The kingdom of God has come near.'

All eyes were locked on him.

'Change your hearts and your lives – and believe!'

And that was it.

From that moment on, everything started to change. And everywhere we went, people followed.

30

The Touch

MY BEST MOMENTS were always when it was just us – a handful of his followers, just closest friends, and Yeshua.

We would often spend the evenings sitting on the shore of the Sea of Galilee, a fire lit, fish grilling, laughing, joshing each other – and often ribbing Yeshua too. He was easy to mimic.

It was at these sorts of times that Yeshua seemed happiest. No pressures. No demands.

But those times were becoming rarer.

Often, a whole village or town would be trailing after him. For us, it was a strange dynamic. On the one hand, it was exhilarating, and some of the fishermen ended up like bodyguards for him; they enjoyed it. But on the other hand, the crowds were relentless, and they took him away from us.

More and more, we just wanted to spend time alone with him.

He had that effect on people.

It was still my nature to hang back a bit, especially when he was surrounded by people. I preferred to observe from a distance. I liked to see the whole picture. I was never one for getting carried away.

It was why moments like this one stick with me so strongly – because I had witnessed the crowd and the chaos from among it. As I was busy trying to extract myself.

There must have been a hundred people jostling and pushing around him as we walked through this village. It seemed that word had travelled fast that Yeshua was in town, and everyone was out to get a glimpse of the man that so many people were talking about.

The noise of the crowd was so loud it was hard to think.

Some of the other followers were yelling at people to keep back and give the master some room.

And that's when I saw her.

She looked old, but I reckon she was younger than she appeared. She was obviously poor, just from her appearance. She was dressed in an old shawl and her skin was etched with furrows and pain. She had trouble walking and it was clear that every step was a battle.

She was moving along at the very back of the crowd and was desperately trying to find a way through to Yeshua. But it was proving impossible. She was too weak and kept getting repelled by the sheer number of people in the crowd.

When Yeshua paused and turned to talk with someone, the crowd swayed and surged around him. As people shifted position to get a better view, a small gap opened behind him, and this woman didn't wait.

She scuttled forward, back bent, eyes locked on Yeshua.

When she had got as close as she was possibly able, she bent over even further and lunged past the last few people crowded in around Yeshua.

I was the opposite side of Yeshua but could see the bony hand she stretched out towards him. She barely managed to touch the hem of his cloak, and the touch of her finger on cloth only lasted a heartbeat.

But it was enough.

Instantly she pulled back, away from the crowd. I tried to see where she was going, and then spotted her having fallen back behind the surging crowd. But she wasn't shuffling in pain like she had before. She was standing straight up, staring back towards where Yeshua was.

Her face was raised to the sky, shining with joy and wet with tears.

Then I noticed Yeshua had stopped his conversation and was silent. Everyone simmered down and waited for him to speak.

He then called out in a clear voice, 'Who touched my robe?'

It was an odd question for the crowd to hear.

'What are you talking about?' Andreas replied to him. 'With this crowd like this? Everyone's touching you.'

But Yeshua wanted to know who had touched him. He asked the question again.

I kept my eye on the woman. I had seen it all. And now she was looking terrified. She was trying to blend into the crowd again. To hide. All the light had drained from her face.

Once more, Yeshua called out the question. The crowd stopped pushing and started to give him space to look around.

Slowly, the woman took a step forward. Then another. Meekly edging towards Yeshua.

When she was within reach of him, she dropped onto her knees. She was sobbing and she was trying to explain.

She told him that she had been bleeding for twelve years. Doctors had tricked her out of all her money, and she had lost all hope.

Then she had heard about Yeshua. She was desperate.

'I thought, if I could only put a finger on your robe, I would get well.'

She was trembling by this point.

Yeshua bent down and put his head close to hers. The crowd watched on in anticipation.

Just like with the Samaritan woman, Yeshua's face was bright with compassion. As if somehow, he knew every moment of her pain, all that she had been through.

'Daughter,' he said, 'you took a risk of faith, and now you're healed and whole. Live well. Be healed of your plague!'

She slowly stood up and the colour flooded back into her face. The tears continued to fall as she hugged Yeshua, and the crowd cheered.

Even my eyes pricked with emotion at that point. It's hard to fake raw emotion like I was seeing on this woman's face. We all knew something amazing had happened to her. Something beautiful.

To me though, it was still not an undeniable miracle, at least as far as my cynical brain could decipher. To me, it didn't mean Yeshua really was God himself. After all, people stage healing hoaxes all the time.

But something . . . something was happening. In me, in all

of us close to him, and with everyone who came into contact with this extraordinary human being.

And this sort of encounter was starting to happen a lot.

When he was with people, I guess he just couldn't help himself. Always wanting to make people whole and well. Inside and out. Always affirming, nudging us all towards love, towards mercy and towards the light. And he did this in so many little ways, all day long.

It was just incredible to be a part of it all.

As for Yeshua, he wasn't interested in the adulation. As soon as moments like this happened, he tended to want to retreat with us, to get away again. As was his way.

31

Rejected

AS I PREDICTED, news of how Yeshua had healed the official's son spread far and wide.

Even when we headed back to his sleepy hometown of Nazaret, people had heard about it. The whole place turned out to greet him when we arrived, and he was swept into the synagogue so they could hear whatever he had to say.

But that's where my predictions stopped being right.

I'd thought that Yeshua would have a plan to start small, keeping far away from the gaze of Roman soldiers or religious elites. And when that local support was big enough, he'd march into Yerushalayim and demand real change.

I was so wrong.

It all started out so well at the synagogue. All eyes were on Yeshua as he stood up to teach them. He spoke simply of love and compassion to one another. About honouring God and each other.

People loved it, and started nodding and speaking their approval.

'Yeshua the stonemason, the son of Myriam . . . Where did he get such wisdom? And we have his cousins and family still here with us.'

That sentiment didn't last long.

Yeshua then stood up once more. This time more formally, and everyone went silent before him. People were crowded around wanting to hear more.

Yeshua was handed the scroll of the prophet Isaiah. He found the place he was after and then started to read aloud:

'God's Spirit is on me; he's chosen me to preach the message of good news to the poor. To set the burdened and battered free. To announce, "This is God's time to shine!"'

Then he spoke these words: 'You've just heard Scripture make history. It came true just now in this place.'

He then rolled up the scroll, handed it back to the assistant and looked across at everyone with a piercing stare. Every eye in the place was on him, intent. Everyone was hoping for some words of divine affirmation for his local town, for the faithful chosen.

Instead, Yeshua gave it to them straight: 'You will tell me: "Do here in your hometown what we have heard that you did in Kfar Nahum."' He paused.

'Truly I tell you, no prophet is accepted in his hometown.'

The atmosphere turned in an instant. From comfortable self-congratulations to chaos.

Everyone suddenly started talking, their voices tumbling over one another.

The main elder was standing now, furious. 'Are you, Yeshua, passing judgement on all of us? Judging us as lacking in faith?'

It seemed he, and many, couldn't contain their shock about Yeshua challenging their lack of faith.

The elder continued. 'Only God can judge us. Or are you the great prophet that Moses promised? Are you the voice of the Almighty now? How dare you!'

Some of them were mocking and saying, 'You're speaking above your station, Yosef's boy.'

Everyone was on their feet, voices raised, and the anger was building.

'We have never heard such arrogance. Just remember what you came from, builder.' The words spat out of the religious elder.

I was backing out of there fast, but there was no escaping the surge of the crowd.

Yeshua had somehow stirred up the ultimate hornet's nest among this religious home crowd, and it wasn't looking good.

In a matter of minutes, they had Yeshua roughly herded out of the synagogue and down towards the edge of the village, where the ground falls away into a steep valley below.

The crowd was incensed.

It felt like everything was unravelling faster than I could keep up with. The same villagers who had been happily nodding their heads at the start, and congratulating themselves on having helped raise such a remarkable man, were now chasing him towards a cliff.

They wanted blood.

Yeshua was right in the middle of the crowd now, being forced along towards the valley edge. I ran alongside, trying to keep up. It was only when the crowd reached the actual cliff itself that the hordes pulled back a little.

Yeshua was only a few steps from the precipice now. One push and he would be gone.

Then he turned back to face them.

He had this expression that I didn't expect to see at all.

The message in his eyes was unmistakable: *do not mess with me.*

The crowd sensed it, and shrank back, just a fraction.

Yeshua took one confident step towards them, away from the cliff edge.

They moved back again.

He took one more step, then shook his cloak and walked steadily away from them, along the cliff edge, towards the less steep ground.

Without a backward glance, he then headed out of Nazaret, with us scuttling along behind.

None of us spoke a word. It had been a traumatic moment, and for a while I couldn't make up my mind how I felt about what had happened in his hometown.

I loved the way he stood up to the mob and stared them down, but I couldn't understand why he had let it get to that stage in the first place.

He had them in the palm of his hand when he was teaching them in the synagogue and reading from the scrolls.

Why did he have to wind them up like that?

It was as if every time that anyone felt like they had figured him out, myself included, he showed another layer to who he was.

Like he was cleverly undoing everything that we had got wrong about God. And it made many people very uncomfortable.

Truth can be like that sometimes.

32

Demonic Powers

AFTER THINGS GOT heated in Nazaret, we set off on a journey like no other across Galilee.

Yeshua was relentless, and in the same way that Yohanan's arrest gave him a reason to speak publicly, I think that the rejection he experienced in his hometown made him want to visit as many different towns and villages in the region as possible.

We spent a lot of time down by the lake, even adding a few more fishermen to our number. Then, just when I thought I was beginning to have him all figured out, Yeshua surprised me again.

He headed straight back to Kfar Nahum and walked right into the synagogue.

It was Shabbat again, our holy day, and just like at Nazaret, he started teaching. I won't lie, I was nervous, and quietly planning our escape if things turned sour.

But this time was different. He talked with authority, talking about God in ways the people could understand. And the more Yeshua spoke, the more intrigued they were.

'If you judge others, you will be judged the same way you judge them. God will treat you the same way you treat others.'

It was beautiful, simple, relevant teaching.

'Why do you notice the small piece of dust that is in your friend's eye, but you don't notice the big piece of wood that is in your own? Look at yourself first!' He paused and looked around him.

'First, take the wood out of your own eye. Then you will see clearly to get the dust out of your friend's eye.'

By the time he stopped, the synagogue was full of regular people just listening. Many, I thought, were the sort who would not normally be in the synagogue. It was something about the way he spoke using stories or pictures, and each one relevant to everyday struggles and lives.

Just then, a man stood up and started screaming wildly at Yeshua. It was a terrifying, screeching voice.

'Yeshua of Nazaret! I know who you are. You are God's Holy One!'

The man was crazed. His whole body was shaking as he held his hand out, pointing accusingly at Yeshua.

'What do you want with us?' the man screamed. 'Did you come to destroy us?'

I felt trouble building. I was convinced that things were about to unravel just like they had before. But unlike in Nazaret, Yeshua did not stay silent. Instead, he got to his feet and looked hard at the man.

When he spoke, his voice was louder and stronger than I'd ever heard it.

'Be quiet and come out of him!'

The man's shaking suddenly got a hundred times worse. His limbs were thrashing out violently and his eyes rolled back into his head. Then there was a massive scream, and it appeared as if something almost exploded out of him.

The man collapsed to the floor, and was now lying limp, gently heaving for breath. His shaking then soon stopped. Silence fell throughout the synagogue.

For a moment, everybody stared at the man on the floor and at Yeshua crouching down beside him.

'What is happening?' someone called out. 'He commands evil spirits, and they obey him?'

The crowds surged in, people talking excitedly, everyone pressing in around Yeshua. No one had ever seen anything like it.

If you'd asked me before whether demonic powers were real, I would have told you not to be so foolish. But I know what I saw. The man had been possessed. But when Yeshua had told those spirits to leave, the demons had instantly obeyed.

I'd never seen anything so powerful, and terrifying, in all my life.

33

Healed, Restored

WHEN WE LEFT the synagogue, we hurried to the home of Shimon's mother-in-law. She had been taken ill and Shimon had been fretting about her all day.

Yeshua had promised to visit her straight away.

The fever had been getting worse and worse, and Shimon's wife sat beside her mother's bed, wiping her brow with a cool cloth. Shimon was pacing the outer room worriedly.

For a big burly fisherman, he was as gentle to his mother-in-law as anyone I'd ever seen. He'd do anything for her. We often ribbed him about it.

But today was not a good day. And Shimon, and those of us who then saw his mother-in-law, could understand why. We were all genuinely worried for her life.

By the time Yeshua finally arrived, Shimon and his wife were in a blind panic and the fever was getting worse still.

Yeshua calmly walked straight up to the woman's bedside and took her hand in his. By now, she was pale and sweaty, and struggling to breathe. Her cheeks were sunken, and her chest was going up and down in shallow gasps.

I was sure that death was hovering nearby.

Yeshua did nothing for a while. He just stood there, holding her hand, looking tenderly at her in silence.

We all waited, wondering what he was doing.

Then she opened her eyes, and Yeshua smiled and motioned for her to get up.

I thought that was a mistake.

She had been too weak to breathe a moment ago, let alone now stand up. But suddenly, she eased herself to her feet and allowed Yeshua to support her on her shaky legs. In front of us, we could almost see the fever leave her body. And just like that, she was better.

Restored to full strength and health.

She smiled, looked around her a little surprised, then took a deep breath and chuckled.

I couldn't believe it. Nor could Shimon and his wife, who both rushed forward and held her hands to check she really was all right.

'Are you sure you feel all right?' Shimon asked in awe. 'What are you feeling?'

'I feel just fine,' she replied, and then she hugged Shimon and her daughter, before then turning to hug Yeshua.

Everyone was laughing and some were crying. Shimon included. (And trust me, you don't often see that.)

These sort of encounters, of unexplainable things just happening in a heartbeat, were getting ever more frequent. And a little part of me had simply stopped trying to figure out how he was doing this.

Sometimes you can analyse things to death and then miss the beauty in front of you.

So, I told myself, *Just soak it all up. Stay alert, don't get too carried away and see where all this leads.*

After all, I figured if it was all real, then we were in the perfect place. And if it wasn't real, then it would soon all unravel anyway. Life has a way of operating like that. Truth tends to come out eventually.

It obviously wasn't the first extraordinary thing that Yeshua had done, but it was one of my favourites. I liked the fact that it was away from the crowds, and that only a handful of people saw it. It was silent and it was private, and so beautifully consistent with who Yeshua always said he was.

Other miraculous moments weren't so easy to watch.

One day, we were walking near a cemetery when two men suddenly stepped out into the road ahead of us. They were covered in cuts and scabs and looked like they wanted either to rob us or kill us. They appeared crazed, and were laughing and spitting.

Little did we know at the time, but these men had been

terrorising that stretch of road for some time – so much so that locals had started simply avoiding going anywhere near the cemetery.

As they moved towards us, we were instantly on edge.

But Yeshua just stepped forward.

As soon as the men saw him, they started screaming, throwing their bodies on the ground and twisting in the dust. It was terrifying to see, and the voice and screams reminded me of the man in the synagogue the other day.

Both these men seemed riddled with violence and hate, and as they leapt around, one of them started hitting the ground deliriously.

If ever I had imagined demonic spirits, this is what they looked like.

I couldn't help but drop back discreetly, behind Yeshua.

The men then started shouting at Yeshua in crazed voices.

'What business do you have giving us a hard time? You're the Son of God! You weren't supposed to show up here yet!'

I looked at Shimon and he shrugged, eyes wide as well. We all edged a little closer together.

One of the voices then begged Yeshua, 'If you kick us out of these men, let us live in the pigs.'

Yeshua then looked across the hillside to our right, and we could see there was a herd of pigs grazing and rooting. Yeshua nodded calmly.

The two scabby men then shook violently once more, before suddenly being released of whatever had been inside them.

The men lay there on the ground, groaning gently, then they slowly started to get to their feet. They seemed totally different people. New.

In a second, we all then heard the pigs start squealing and running around madly. We stood there and watched as they charged straight towards a cliff.

And then they ran right over the edge.

We stood there speechless.

We then noticed a group of locals who had been cautiously watching the whole commotion from a distance behind us. They appeared to have seen everything that had happened.

Yet when they saw the whole herd of pigs destroyed, they started shouting at us furiously, blaming us and shouting at us to leave.

So, we did.

And to be honest, I didn't blame them.

I wasn't going back there in a hurry.

34

Be Clean

FROM THAT POINT on, everywhere we went the crowds got ever bigger. And they were growing week by week.

People had heard about what happened in Kfar Nahum with the official's son, and in the synagogue with the man possessed, and so many other moments like these. More than I was able to keep track of.

Everyone wanted to bring the sick and disabled to Yeshua.

The more people he touched and helped, the bigger the crowds became.

Soon, wherever we were staying, there would be people waiting outside in the morning. And often all night too. It was intense to be a part of.

They'd be huddled up together, patiently waiting for Yeshua to wake up and begin his work among them.

As for my scepticism, it was becoming harder and harder for me to deny that what I was seeing was miraculous. I just kept coming up short for explanations. And trust me, I tried.

We travelled all over the region. Everywhere we went, Yeshua appeared to be casting out demons, breaking fevers and healing paralysed limbs. Everyone went wild for him.

It was an incredible time, and even though the days rushed by in a blur of crowds, sickness, tears and laughter, there were always moments within them that stood out.

Like the time a man with severe leprosy knelt before Yeshua. And, of course, the crowd instantly recoiled, keeping their distance. Sickness or disability is one thing. Leprosy though, for us all, is something that you simply don't mess with.

We had all been taught since childhood to avoid contact with a leper at all costs, and the fear of catching leprosy is all too real. Everyone in the crowd that day knew that you get too close to a leper at your own risk. And the cost is often perilously high.

Lepers are considered so unclean, and their disfigurement so disgusting, that they are banished from entering towns or villages. They can't work, they are separated from their families and friends, and they get confined to leper colonies in an often futile attempt to keep their uncleanliness contained.

And as they approach anyone, they are forced to ring a bell and shout in a loud voice, as a warning, 'Unclean . . . Unclean!' The sound of this is enough to instil fear into the hearts of anyone nearby. Trust me.

Life as a leper is brutal.

It means complete separation and isolation, followed by a slow decline to death, riddled with scabs, deformities and weeping sores.

And we had all heard the horror stories of limbs and fingers of lepers simply falling off, as they got infected and decomposed before the leper's very eyes.

It was hard not to be shocked when we saw this leper. His face was like molten wax and his fingers were either missing or misshapen.

He stood there alone. A pariah to the town. People were shouting at him to get away.

But what did Yeshua do?

He stepped forward. Close to the man. And let the leper speak.

'Master,' he said, 'if you want to, you can heal my body.'

Yeshua knelt, reached out a hand and touched the leper. Not on the filthy rags that covered his back. He touched his hand. Then Yeshua touched his head. Skin on skin. Clean on unclean.

'I want to,' Yeshua whispered. 'Be clean.'

As soon as the words had left Yeshua's mouth, the leprosy just seemed to melt away, in front of our eyes. The broken skin, the lesions, the warts, they just vanished. As if they had just dissolved away in a second, like salt swirled in water.

The leprosy wasn't just reduced or eased. Not gradually receded or slowly healing over. It was just gone. His skin was clear, bright and whole, the tips of his fingers were restored.

The leper stood there dumbfounded; eyes wide open in shock. He was feeling his arms and stroking his face with his hands. Clear. Clean. He started rapidly feeling all over his body and tearing his bandages away to check. Everything was as new. Smooth. Restored.

Right there, before a hundred pairs of eyes. The leper had been made like new. Nobody could quite believe what they had seen.

The whole crowd gasped. Their faces all turned to Yeshua.

Others were just standing there and shaking their head in amazement. Then the shouting and the cheers of joy erupted.

Once the crowd started, it sounded like they would never stop. The hands reached out, and the people surged towards Yeshua.

It was the most beautiful chaos you could ever imagine.

35

Get Up and Walk

A FEW DAYS later, we were back in Kfar Nahum.

We were at Shimon's mother-in-law's house, and we were all tired and wanting to rest. But Yeshua was determined to keep going. Talking with whoever came to see him.

I sometimes wondered how he kept it up. It was like he had this endless strength of will to be there for whoever asked for him.

Yeshua sat down on the floor, listening, and teaching, and laying his hands on many children's heads and blessing them. He loved to do this. It was the one thing that seemed to give him energy rather than drain it from him.

The house was full of people now, all just hoping to get a glimpse of Yeshua for themselves.

I had never seen the place so rammed. Not one more person could have got inside, but even that didn't stop others.

I spotted one group of young men, who had been shouting earlier outside the door, start to climb up onto the roof.

Shimon shouted at them to get down, but the youths took no notice. Then suddenly, they hauled back the thatch on the roof and widened a hole big enough to lower down a stretcher.

We all then watched this mat descend, with a paralysed man bundled up inside it.

Yeshua was smiling at the brazen audacity of the paralysed man's friends, and before the figure had even hit the ground, Yeshua told him with a smile, 'Young man, your sins are forgiven.'

Forgiving this man's sins?

That took us all by surprise.

And the comment didn't go unnoticed.

Some of the rabbis who were there started muttering disapproval, calling such language: blasphemy.

'Who is this man to say such things?' they whispered. 'Can a mere man forgive sins against God? Just like that?'

But as usual, Yeshua was ahead of them.

Right there, in the middle of the house that had grown so hot it was hard to breathe, Yeshua stood up and raised his hands to quieten everyone.

Then he spoke plainly.

'Why this gossipy whispering? Which do you think is simpler: to say, "I forgive your sins," or, "Get up and walk"?'

Yeshua looked around for an answer that he knew would never come.

He continued. 'Well, just so it's clear that I'm the Son of Man and authorised to do either . . .' Yeshua now turned to the paraplegic and said, 'Get up. Take your mat and go home.'

At this, the man put his hands on the floor, bent his knees to his chest, and in one fluid motion he simply stood up.

Everyone burst into spontaneous applause.

The man just stood there though, unable quite to comprehend how he had managed to stand up in such a manner. He was wide-eyed in total shock at himself. Then a huge smile broke across his face, and he looked up to his friends and started to dance. Everyone burst into laughter and started cheering, none more loudly than his friends who were waving their arms in excitement from the hole in the roof.

Even the rabbis were surprised and looked at each other in stunned disbelief.

That day, a true celebration of life and laughter came to that household.

Whenever I think back to those days, travelling throughout Galilee, I smile to myself. The long walks, the nights together under the stars. The miraculous events, the hungry crowds. Then the retreating into the hills, just us all together. Followed by endless fishing on the lake, and endless laughter.

Even I, the old cynic that I was, began to laugh more. And occasionally I was talked into joining Shimon, Andreas and the others in a few mugs of rough wine.

In time, so much would change. The crowds wouldn't always be so full of love, and the teachers of the law wouldn't be silenced so easily. But back then, it was like a golden time. A period where everything was full of light. And the darkness could not penetrate it.

My greatest hope was that it might stay that way forever.

It didn't.

It couldn't.

36

Back to the City

TROUBLE BREWS QUICKLY.

Especially when people who have power start to see you as a threat.

That's why I was so concerned when Yeshua invited Levi, a tax collector, to join us. It seemed like a bad idea to me. And inflammatory to many.

'Follow me,' Yeshua had said to him. We were surprised, to say the least. But just like that, the tax man simply got up, left everything and followed.

That was the effect Yeshua had on people. On all of us.

That evening, Levi held a banquet for Yeshua at his house, and a large crowd including other tax collectors was there. Some Pharisees and the teachers of the law also came along to see what was happening.

I was aware of the Pharisees – many of whom were devout and dedicated to maintaining standards and the law. But not all the Pharisees were simply prepared to stand by and watch.

Some began to air their concerns at the company that Yeshua was keeping.

'Why do you eat and drink with tax collectors and sinners?' one of them asked him.

Everyone stopped to listen.

Yeshua answered simply, 'It is not the healthy who need a doctor, but the sick. I have not come to call the righteous, but sinners.'

And that was that. The Pharisee turned and walked away.

Many Pharisees had made it clear they were not in need of rescuing, not by some Galilean builder.

Despite the grumblings about Yeshua eating with tax collectors and traitors, it didn't affect the numbers of people crowding around us always. There was still an endless stream of people pleading with Yeshua for help.

But trouble was brewing all the same.

Powerful people were beginning to take notice of Yeshua – and some even started sending spies to keep an eye on him.

These powerful people weren't just Romans though, or other tax collectors. It was now the priests and religious leaders who were starting to monitor what Yeshua was saying and doing.

It appeared that they were the ones who felt most threatened by him and his teaching. As if Yeshua was upsetting the status quo of religious formalities – not to mention threatening the hidden backhanders and privileges that many were benefitting from.

Personally, I'd have preferred us to have stayed in Galilee and continued Yeshua's ministry around there. He could have continued to help and heal people in the region, under the radar, and it probably would have kept a lid on trouble.

But who was I to tell him what to do?

Yeshua didn't want to hide away. He wanted to engage with the religious leaders, and he wanted to shine his light on everyone.

And so, we headed south. To Yerushalayim.

Almost a whole year had passed since we had last been in the city. It seemed like a lifetime had gone by since we had sat with Nicodemus, as he struggled to understand what Yeshua meant by being born anew.

Back then, nobody noticed us when we arrived, but now there were spies everywhere. I could sense them.

Everything Yeshua did and said was reported back to the priests. Not that it seemed to bother him. It was as if he wanted the religious leaders to be paying attention to him.

Yeshua didn't waste any time.

Near the Sheep Gate in the city, there is a pool, called Bethesda, with five alcoves. Hundreds of sick people – blind, crippled, paralysed – would gather in these alcoves.

One man there had been an invalid for thirty-eight years. When Yeshua saw him stretched out by the water, he simply said to him, 'Do you want to get well?'

The man nodded frantically.

Yeshua reached down and touched his hand, telling him, 'Get up, take your bedroll, start walking.'

And just like that, the man got to his feet and started to move freely – full use of every limb and muscle.

Soon he was dancing, shocked, staring wide-eyed around in disbelief. The man could move everything. He spun on the spot, laughing, then clung to the hands of Yeshua and started kissing them.

I shook my head in amazement. Not for the first time.

There was one other factor to this apparent miracle.

It was Shabbat. The official religious day of rest.

Yeshua remained at the temple, as if waiting for the inevitable visit from the priests. It didn't take long for them to show.

They were mad, and demanded to know why he was breaking the law and going about his work on Shabbat. They even told him to stop helping people.

Yeshua roared with laughter at that.

'My Father never stops working, and so I work too.'

You could see the anger and frustration on their faces.

But Yeshua wouldn't back down.

Instead, letting the whole gathering settle and the murmuring die down, he spoke once more, clearly and with purpose:

'I tell you, whoever hears my word and believes him who sent me has eternal life.'

There was an intensity now that everyone could feel.

Yeshua paused.

Then he looked around, smiled and raised his hands.

'They have already left death and have entered into life.'

Such words were going to stir up a hornet's nest. I knew it.

37

Shabbat

ALL THROUGH THE next week, the spies were out in force. They joined whatever crowd was following us – watching and listening intently to every word Yeshua uttered.

And he was talking a lot.

He talked about being the Son of God. That he was offering eternal life.

He even criticised the priests themselves, accusing them of studying Scriptures but blindly ignoring everything within them that pointed to Yeshua as the Messiah.

Yet despite all this, the priests didn't pounce.

They were waiting for something concrete, irrefutable and public.

They got what they wanted one Shabbat.

We were walking through a field – being followed by a few people who had clearly been sent by the religious elite – when one of us picked some wheat and started eating the grains within.

It was nothing to most people, but to the religious 'police' it was a clear offence – and a deliberate breaking of the law.

When it came to the experts in Jewish law, it always seemed to me that small offences were big offences, and the deeper offences of the heart were often ignored.

An hour or so later, when we were back in the city, a group of priests marched up to Yeshua. They were tense from the start, jabbing their fingers and making out that they were shocked and appalled by what had happened.

They wanted him to explain why he had let his followers break the Shabbat law and pick grain.

There was a small crowd around us by now, watching and listening. I wasn't enjoying this at all. It was a clear set-up.

But Yeshua got to the heart of the matter.

'Shabbat was made to help people. People were not made to be ruled by Shabbat.'

Some of the people listening at the back gave a small cheer of approval. We all felt the same. Who wasn't tired of the constant debates and disagreements over legal observance, when everyone deep down knew that Yeshua was right?

The priests didn't like his response. Such a nonchalant remark was in direct opposition to everything they stood for. And they weren't finished.

'Your followers don't even follow the traditions we have from our great leaders who lived long ago. They eat their food with hands that are not clean. Why?'

Yeshua shook his head. It was now his time to lose patience.

'You are all hypocrites,' he shouted.

The crowd froze. He was brimming with fury now.

'You have stopped following God's commands, preferring instead the man-made rules you get from others.'

The priests were certainly not used to being spoken to like this. Not by a poor, itinerant teacher from a rural backwater like Galilee.

They looked like they'd just been slapped.

But Yeshua didn't stop there.

He walked over to the synagogue and strode right in.

Just like before, he paused and looked around until his eyes rested on someone who needed healing. There was a man with a crippled hand, his wrist hanging awkwardly at a strange angle, deformed. The man shuffled towards Yeshua.

Everyone sensed the confrontation that was about to happen.

One of the priests goaded Yeshua.

'So?' He paused, looking at Yeshua. 'Is it legal to heal on Shabbat?'

Yeshua took the bait and let the line run.

'Is there a person here who, finding one of your lambs fallen into a ravine, wouldn't, even though it was Shabbat, pull it out?'

Nobody spoke.

Yeshua was staring at them, his eyes full of fire and mischief.

'Surely kindness to people is as legal as kindness to animals?'

Again, nobody answered him.

So, he turned to the man.

'Hold out your hand,' he said.

The man did. Then the man looked down at it – and gasped.

His hand and wrist had been instantly healed. The bones restored – straight and strong. The skin fresh and new. The man shrieked and started waving his arm and caressing and stroking his wrist. He stood there shaking his head in confusion and staring at Yeshua.

Yeshua smiled at the man then turned on his heels and walked away.

We hurried to catch up with him.

I looked back at the priests and the Pharisees. Some were standing silently, deep in thought, wondering if somehow this might all be true.

Others appeared convinced it was trickery.

One had thrown his cloak on the floor and was stamping on it.

He was shouting at Yeshua. 'I will expose you for the deceiver and the false prophet you are.' He paused. Then shouted even louder. 'Your days are numbered.'

For once, I had a feeling they were telling the truth.

38

Divine Truths

WE LEFT YERUSHALAYIM as soon as the Passover celebrations were over, heading north towards Kfar Nahum. I was happy to be out of the city, walking for hours along dry tracks, stopping beneath shaded trees when the sun was at its hottest.

We knew there would still be spies up ahead in the larger villages and towns, but the journey itself was a gift. After the chaos of Passover, I couldn't get enough of the silence and the stillness.

I loved those days spent travelling with Yeshua. Listening to him talk as we walked alongside him, they were always the times when I felt closest to him.

No pressures. Just walking and talking and being together.

Things returned to a more normal footing the further north we travelled. There were still lots of people coming to see Yeshua whenever we stopped in a village, and just like before, the crowds were growing.

As ever, Yeshua would spend his time with the sick, the lonely and the marginalised, and he would always talk of forgiveness and kindness.

The message never got old. If anything, it felt new every time.

Little did I know that what I was about to hear were, arguably, the greatest words ever spoken by a man. I was woefully unprepared for their power – or what they would demand of me.

Yeshua was the most unpredictable man I'd ever met, and it was impossible to guess his next move. But I had seen enough of him by now to know that everything he did and everything he said had a reason, even if I couldn't understand it at first.

We were a few days out of Yerushalayim – just the usual group of followers, as well as a few others who had joined us that day.

We were heading towards a small town when we suddenly spotted a crowd of people up ahead. I guessed it was at least a hundred strong.

Yeshua stood looking across at them, and then he simply turned and headed up the hill to our side.

We all looked at him and then at each other. Then we followed on in silence, a little surprised. The crowd soon followed too, trying desperately to catch up with him.

Yeshua was going to make them work for what was coming.

Then finally, when he was just beneath the crest of a small ravine, with everyone crowded in beneath him, he turned and stopped.

Yeshua slowly raised a hand and beckoned us to sit down.

He stood silent for some time, and we sat waiting. Then he took a deep breath, raised his hands and spoke words of life to us all.

Yeshua began in prayer: 'Thank you, Father, Lord of heaven and earth. You've concealed your ways from sophisticates and know-it-alls, but spelled them out clearly to ordinary people. . .'

He lowered his head, opened his eyes and started to talk to us.

'Are you tired? Worn out? Burned out on religion? Come to me.' His eyes shone as if on fire. As if he had wanted to speak these truths to us for so long.

'Get away with me and you'll recover your life. I'll show you how to take a real rest. Walk with me and work with me – watch how I do it. Learn the unforced rhythms of grace.' There was a calm urgency in his tone.

'I won't lay anything heavy or ill-fitting on you. Keep company with me and you'll learn to live freely and lightly.'

He paused and breathed in deeply. Time seemed to stand still. Then he stretched out his hands, smiled and the words fell from his lips upon us:

'Blessed are the poor in spirit, for theirs is the kingdom of heaven.' He paused.

'Blessed are those who mourn, for they will be comforted.'

Yeshua looked around at all those gathered beneath him, and I noticed that his eyes were now wet with tears.

He then took a few steps down towards the crowd, so that he was now among them as he spoke. Men, women, children sat on rocks, listening intently and gathered all around him.

Yeshua held some of their hands now as he spoke.

'Blessed are the meek, for they *will* inherit the earth.'

'Blessed are those who hunger and thirst for righteousness, for they will be filled.'

This was not a conversation. He was not inviting us to respond. This was Yeshua setting humanity straight.

He wasn't turning things upside down, as I had often thought he was doing. He was putting things the right way up again.

It felt as if his words had somehow been beautifully crafted and planned since the dawn of ages. Words that were not instructions of what to do or how to be; but words that were a statement of what was happening.

The great re-fresh.

Words of life for a fallen world.

For the struggling, the marginalised, for those on the back foot. For those in pain or forgotten. Yeshua was reminding us all – the abused, the weak, the impoverished and the devastated – that the kingdom of heaven is truly ours.

He smiled at a small child and ruffled his hair.

'Blessed are the pure in heart, for they will see God.'

I was listening so carefully that I barely noticed my own eyes were wet with tears too.

Then Yeshua looked at the adults and the elders among the crowd.

'Blessed are the merciful, for they will be shown mercy.'

'Blessed are the peacemakers, for they will be called children of God.'

The words just kept pouring forth from him. Guidance on everything. From life and families, to fears, worries and our futures. I remember he spoke about being salt of the earth. And light to the world.

People sat enthralled and they drank it all in, like I had never witnessed before.

'You have heard that it was said, "Eye for eye, and tooth for tooth."' He continued. 'But I tell you, do not resist an evil person. If anyone slaps you on the right cheek, turn to them the other cheek also.'

What Yeshua was demanding of us here was a tough ask.

People started to look around, unsure of themselves. But Yeshua persevered.

'You have heard that it was said, "Love your neighbour and hate your enemy." But I tell you, love your enemies and pray for those who persecute you, that you may be children of your Father in heaven.'

What is he asking us? To love the Romans?

I felt Yeshua was drifting into a place that many of us could not follow. But he didn't temper his message. He let it all flow out.

'For I tell you that unless your righteousness surpasses that of the Pharisees and the teachers of the law, you will certainly not enter the kingdom of heaven.'

And right there, I knew we were all in trouble.

How radically he was asking us to live and love.

It was a standard none of us could reach.

39

Stone's Throw

I WAS CONCERNED that Yeshua had just set humanity a benchmark for holiness, for access into his kingdom, that no one on earth would ever be able to attain.

But I didn't want to flag this to Yeshua.

Maybe I should have.

I should have remembered that Yeshua liked it when people questioned him. He loved the chance to challenge lazy thinking. And he was always happy to play along and let those of us who were intrigued discover truths for ourselves.

Not everyone liked the theological tussles.

In fact, some of those closest to Yeshua found his words confusing and refused to take the bait. I often remember Shimon checking out of a conversation, getting to his feet and just going fishing.

I admired his honesty.

But Yeshua liked to get people to a place where they had serious questions, so that he could then reveal the truth of who he was.

With me, it took a while. But Yeshua eventually did it in the most amazing way. Just when I least expected it.

We were once more in Yerushalayim, back in the temple. By now, the crowds were larger than ever before – to the point it was getting difficult to hear him teach.

But on this day, it wasn't Yeshua who was doing the talking.

It was the Pharisees.

They were standing there, flowing robes on display for all to see – and to revere.

But their faces were like thunder as they strutted towards Yeshua.

And they were not alone.

Behind them was a terrified looking woman. She had two temple guards either side of her. Her face was bruised and her clothes were torn.

The woman was violently hurled down onto the dirt in front of Yeshua. For a moment nobody spoke.

Yeshua was looking only at the woman.

I glanced around. There were baskets of stones and coils of thick rope nearby. That only meant one thing.

This woman was about to be stoned to death.

I wanted to run, but the crowds were so thick that it was hard to retreat. And there was a palpable taste for blood in the air. People were hungry for violence, and as far as this crowd was concerned, this woman deserved it.

Yet Yeshua looked so calm.

I just hoped that he knew what he was doing.

'Teacher,' the lead Pharisee said, his voice booming so that everyone could hear. 'This woman was caught red-handed in the act of adultery. Moses, in the law, gives orders to such persons.'

He paused for effect.

'They are to be stoned until death.'

40

Who Condemns You?

'DO YOU NOT agree with our forefathers?' The Pharisee looked around confidently. He knew he was on solid ground.

He said it again: 'This woman was caught red-handed in the act of adultery. Moses gives orders to such persons . . . They are to be stoned until death.'

The Pharisee looked at Yeshua, waiting for an answer.

'Do you not have anything to say?'

It was the most obvious trap I'd ever seen.

To entice Yeshua to say something that they could use against him.

Yeshua did not say a word.

He just knelt and started writing in the dirt with his finger.

'Teacher!' the Pharisee bellowed once more, his voice now dripping with sarcasm. 'What do you say we should do with her? Let her go and defy Moses himself?'

Yeshua remained crouched down, gently toying with the sand.

The crowd was starting to stir. Then Yeshua finally stood up. He walked slowly over to the pile of rough, sharp stones and paused.

He picked one up and held it out.

Then he spoke in a clear voice to the entire crowd.

'The sinless one among you, go first: throw the stone.'

Nobody moved.

Yeshua turned all around, holding the stone out to everyone nearby.

'The sinless one among you, go first,' he repeated. 'Throw the stone.'

He even offered it to the Pharisees.

But nobody would take it. People started to look away from his gaze.

The tension was palpable.

Yeshua gently replaced the stone, bent down again and went back to writing in the dirt.

The Pharisees hovered with indecision. The wind was torn from their sails and the crowd sensed it. Some were starting to laugh at them.

Eventually, the Pharisees looked at each other in frustration, turned on their heels, gathered their robes in their hands and stormed off.

People were cheering now.

As for me, I was stunned.

When all the Pharisees and their mob had gone, Yeshua walked over to the woman.

I knew she was safe for now from the Pharisees, with their stones and their lust for power and punishment. But what would Yeshua do and say to her?

If she's been caught in adultery, then sin is sin, and justice is justice.

I kept thinking of the words he'd said in that remote ravine out in the countryside: *Unless your righteousness surpasses that of the Pharisees and the teachers of the law, you will certainly not enter the kingdom of heaven.*

As far as I could tell, that meant she was excluded, and we all were excluded.

Yeshua crouched down beside her and asked, 'Does no one condemn you?'

'No one, Master,' she replied, through her tears.

Yeshua reached for her hand. 'Neither do I. Go on your way. From now on, sin no more.'

That was it.

No sermon. No lecture. Just love and mercy.

I can't even tell you exactly what happened to the crowd – or the woman. I remember her kissing his hands through her sobs, and then getting up and just running away.

The crowds soon dispersed.

That encounter was a pivotal moment for me, because I

started to see that Yeshua was all about restoring people. It was as if he was showing that, ultimately, the world is meant to be complete – to be whole.

When Yeshua healed, or helped, or saved anyone, I started to see it not so much as a miracle, as everyone around us kept saying, but more as him restoring people to how earth was originally meant to be.

No sickness, no hatred, no envy, no cruelty. No power plays. Just love. Light.

'I am the light of the world,' he once told us. 'Whoever lives in me will never live in darkness.'

The words raged like fire inside me.

I began to realise that if Yeshua could somehow truly forgive me and make me right – not just to the level of the Pharisees but to the standard of heaven itself – then such forgiveness would change everything.

He would save the world. Yeshua. 'He who saves.'

But it was a big if. And the Pharisees we kept encountering just couldn't fathom it. Or his authority to speak like this.

'We cannot accept what you say,' I heard one respond. 'You're your own witness! It has no validity.'

I understood their argument. But Yeshua didn't flinch.

'Even if I testify on my own behalf, my testimony is valid, for I know where I came from and where I am going.' Yeshua looked around intensely. 'But you have no idea where I come from or where I am going. You judge by human standards.'

You could hear a pin drop now.

'I stand with the Father, who sent me.'

And at that 'blasphemy', the Pharisees threw their hands in the air in despair once more.

41

Sons and Fathers

AS THE MONTHS passed and I saw more and more of Yeshua in action, both with the crowds and with the Pharisees, I slowly began to understand more of what he was about.

I started really to listen to him.

And what I heard was pure love. Words of life.

One day, we were getting ready to move on to a new town when some Pharisees came up and started talking angrily to us.

Again, they were accusing Yeshua of hanging out with low-life. Spending his time with those who were the despised or rejected. (Which a lot of the time was true. After all, we had seen tax collectors, adulterers, Samaritans and lepers all owe their restored life to Yeshua.)

The Pharisees then accused him of being a glutton and a drunkard.

That made Yeshua roar with laughter.

He responded beautifully, as ever. 'Yohanan came, not eating like other people or drinking wine, and people say, "He has a demon inside him." The Son of Man came eating and drinking, and people say, "Look at him! He eats too much and drinks too much wine. He's a friend of tax collectors and other sinners."'

It appeared Yeshua could not win.

But it felt like they were trying to catch Yeshua out. I didn't like it.

Yeshua watched the Pharisees try to work out their response. But before they could speak, he added:

'But wisdom is shown to be right by what it does.'

And with that he left.

To me and those of us closest to Yeshua, his message was always clear: 'Unless you turn to God you will die.' Yeshua had told us that, plain and simple.

Just as Yohanan had announced at the River Yarden. What I noticed is that regular people, with real needs, loved Yeshua.

That part was undeniable. And our numbers continued to grow.

But so many of the Pharisees appeared to have a blind spot with him: unable to see Yeshua as someone who was restoring people and fulfilling the law, but rather as a troublemaker who kept forgiving the unforgivable and was intent on breaking the law.

Or maybe it was simply that they were the ones who had the most to lose. And it was uncomfortable when Yeshua shone his light on their hearts and their rituals.

Personally, I would have been tempted just to ignore most of the Pharisees, but Yeshua refused to give up on anyone.

Another time, a few days later, and with yet another room full of Pharisees listening in, Yeshua told this story.

It was about a son who rejected his father so badly. In a manner that was as culturally offensive as it was possible to do.

Yeshua began:

'There was once a man who had two sons. The younger said to his father, "Father, I want right now what's coming to me."

'So, the father divided the property between them.

'It wasn't long before the younger son packed his bags and left for a distant country. There, undisciplined and dissipated, he wasted everything he had.

'After he had gone through all his money, there was a bad famine all through that country and he began to feel it. He signed on with a citizen there who assigned him to his fields to slop the pigs. He was so hungry he would have eaten the corncobs in the pig slop, but no one would give him any.

'That brought him to his senses.

'He said, "All those farmhands working for my father sit

down to three meals a day, and here I am starving to death. I'm going back to my father. I'll say to him, 'Father, I've sinned against God, I've sinned before you; I don't deserve to be called your son. Take me on as a hired hand.'"

'He got right up and went home to his father.

'When he was still a long way off, his father saw him. His heart pounding, he ran out, embraced him, and kissed him. The son started his speech: "Father, I've sinned against God, I've sinned before you; I don't deserve to be called your son ever again."

'But the father wasn't listening. He was calling to the servants, "Quick. Bring a clean set of clothes and dress him. Put the family ring on his finger and sandals on his feet. Then get a prize-winning heifer and roast it. We're going to feast! We're going to have a wonderful time!

"My son is here – given up for dead and now alive! Given up for lost and now found!"'

When Yeshua finished the story, everyone was quiet.

Me especially.

The part that struck me most was the father running out to meet his son. The father that would give everything he owned to have his son come home.

The son that had hurt him so much.

Yeshua had told us that the father did not walk. He ran. And then embraced and kissed his son.

I remember thinking that was the part of the story that Yeshua really wanted us to understand. That the story was really about the father's love, more than the son's failing.

And that God will do anything to have his children home.

42

Storm

WHAT HAPPENED NEXT changed everything for me. It was the moment I finally put away all my doubts and scepticism.

It was also a moment when I'd never experienced so much power.

Or so much fear.

We were up in Galilee by the lake. It was evening time and for once there were no crowds with us. Yeshua had climbed into one of Shimon's old fishing boats and invited the rest of us to join him.

The fishermen needed no further encouragement, setting the sail and pushing off. The rest of us lay back on the benches, a mug of local wine in hand, watching the setting sun. After so many months of being so busy, it was beautiful to be able to relax, just us all together.

An hour later, it was starting to get dark, and Yeshua, dead tired, appeared to be dozing in the stern of the small boat.

We let him be.

It had been a long, hot day, that was for certain.

As we headed back to shore, I noticed a change in the wind. Shimon told us this was normal at this time of year. That the winds often race down from the hills and across the water when the temperature cools in the late afternoon.

And he was not wrong.

Because one moment it was a gentle breeze from the south, next it was hitting us in violent gusts from the east. The boat started pitching from side to side, and I couldn't help but throw up.

The fishermen laughed at me. They could not have seemed less bothered by the wind and waves. Routine weather for them. Their nonchalance made me feel a little better, at least.

Shimon was barking orders, and the others were scampering around the boat, reefing the sail and pointing the bow for shore, which was just a mile away now.

I wasn't enjoying this at all, so I curled up out of the weather in the bottom of the boat, alongside Yeshua, and waited for them to get us ashore.

I tried to think of other matters.

But it didn't work.

The winds got stronger, and the waves got higher. Soon the waves were even breaking over the sides, soaking us all.

Almost all the non-sailors among us were throwing up now as well. I say *almost* because there was one of us who didn't appear to be in any way troubled by the storm. It was Yeshua.

He was still lying curled up – dead to the world.

The winds then got dramatically worse. The sail tore in two and giant waves were now pouring in over the side. Soon the whole deck was flooded.

Shimon was suddenly on high alert and was yelling at us to bail out.

It was all I could do to hold on to the side to stay in the boat.

We were pitching so far over that I was convinced we'd all be thrown overboard. I shook Yeshua on the shoulder to wake him. We would need all hands to help if we were going to survive this squall.

But Yeshua didn't stir.

All I was thinking was that we were going to die in this tiny boat.

'Yeshua!' I heard someone yell. 'Don't you care about us? We are going to drown!'

At this, Yeshua slowly lifted his head and looked around lazily. Then he carefully got to his feet, holding on to the side of the boat.

He raised his head, closed his eyes and spoke in a calm, strong voice:

'Quiet.'

For a moment, I thought I had misheard him, the sound of the wind was so violent.

Then he added, 'Be still.'

He looked around at us and a smile spread across his face, as the rain dripped off his beard. And instantly, the winds calmed down. Within a matter of seconds, the waves literally vanished. The storm had simply disappeared.

We all stood there agasp and looked around.

And all we could now see was the moon's reflection on the millpond calm water.

The lake perfectly flat.

Yeshua moved slowly to the front of the boat and sat down, looking back at us. He ran his hands through his long hair.

Then he spoke again. But this time to us.

'Why were you afraid? Do you still have no faith?'

Nobody spoke. How could we?

We just stared at him and then at each other.

Even Shimon, who was never short of a word about the weather or sea state, was as mute as a rock.

The sense of fear, power and awe that I had experienced in the heart of that storm was nothing compared to now.

This was another level.

It was one thing to see Yeshua heal a woman, or make a leper well, or restore a crippled hand, but this? Speaking to a storm, commanding it to stop – at once?

Who is this? I thought. *Even the wind and the waves obey him.*

I will not lie. I was afraid.

Not afraid for my life, like I'd been in the storm. I was afraid because now, there was no room for questions.

No space for wondering if there might be another explanation. Even the wind and the waves were under his control.

Yeshua wasn't just sent by God. He was God.

And that was proving to be quite a discovery.

I thought back on my journey.

How it had all started with that one gulp of wine at the wedding.

Back then, I'd been curious but cautious.

And I stayed that way for the first year that I'd followed Yeshua around. On the edge, observing, questioning, wondering.

Only taking small sips.

It was different now. Because now I knew.

And I wanted in.

I wanted to drink the whole cup of wine.

That night as I lay on the ground, safely ashore, I looked up at the stars, and I realised a simple truth.

It might have been his many miracles that had convinced my head, but it was his love for us and others that had convinced my heart.

PART THREE

Shimon, Fisherman

GALILEE,
C. AD 32

An outlying region of the Roman Empire. A northern trading route, made of poor farming and fishing communities around the lake. Nationalistic. Rebellious.

43

Leave It All

SOME CALL IT impulsive.

But ask any fisherman what it takes to make a living and they'll tell you the same thing: it's instinct. If you can't trust your instincts out there on the water, you might as well pack up and go be a shepherd.

So, when my brother Andreas came and told me he had met someone purporting to be 'the Lamb of God', I was intrigued.

Lamb of God? What did that even mean?

A person to be offered as a sacrifice by God? Sacrificed for what?

It sounded strange.

But Andreas was sharp, and I trusted him.

And I trusted my instinct.

Andreas had loved listening to the wild prophet Yohanan, and it was him who had first pointed out Yeshua to my brother.

And it was Yohanan who had first called him the 'Lamb of God'.

Andreas obviously saw something incredible in this man, Yeshua. He wanted to follow him. And where Andreas went, I went too.

He's my brother, after all.

I just hoped this Yeshua knew what us fishermen were about. We're grafters. We never give up. We speak our mind and we've got the best instincts of anyone alive today.

I'm proud of that.

It's also fair to say that work hadn't been busy for us recently, with the Roman regulations. So, we didn't have a lot to lose.

Still, leaving everything, family, business and my precious boat, was a big decision.

But I figured if it all went wrong, we could always turn around and go back.

All of this meant that Andreas and I were there right at the beginning. We were there at the wedding when Yeshua made that beautiful wine for everyone.

I was there through all those early days when there weren't any crowds.

I was there when royal officials and learned teachers started to seek out Yeshua. For wisdom, healing and revelations.

I saw for myself the miracles, when crippled limbs were restored, lepers were healed, bleeding was stopped and demons were sent packing.

I was sitting right there beside Yeshua the second time we went to the temple for Passover, and I saw him face down many of the Pharisees again and again.

And I was there in the boat when he spoke just two words and calmed the most violent storm that I'd experienced in all my days.

That moment had been incredible.

I'd seen it all. Enough to make me know that he was the One. Enough to make me sure that when it came to Yeshua, I could trust my instincts.

Impulsive or not, I had called this one right.

Still, there have also been a few times when my impulsiveness has got me into trouble.

But we will come to that.

For now, just consider this my story. And be understanding of my mistakes. I'm human. I'm a fisherman. I live with failure in my trade. And at times, I got it very wrong.

What I do know is that with any mistakes I made, Yeshua never once pushed me away. If anything, he only ever seemed to love me more.

I took a punt on him – and he has never let me down.

44

Food for 5,000

FROM THE MOMENT I saw Yeshua that morning, I could tell something was wrong.

We met him down by the lake, and he looked like he had the weight of the world on his shoulders. I'd never seen him so visibly upset.

He told us that his cousin Yohanan the Baptiser had been killed by Antipas, and the news crushed Yeshua.

Yohanan had been held in the dungeons of Antipas for some time, and all of us had been hoping he would soon be released. But it wasn't to be.

Word had it that in a fit of drunken hysteria, Antipas had ordered the head of Yohanan to be brought to him on a platter – to please his new wife Herodias.

His brutality and cowardice knows no bounds it seems.

It took Yeshua a long time to recover from the death of his childhood friend and closest cousin. And in some ways, I don't think he ever got over it. If anything, the death of Yohanan made Yeshua even more focused on completing his mission.

His pace and purpose began to intensify.

And so did the crowds who relentlessly now pursued the man they called the Healer.

I will always remember the time that Yeshua led one of these crowds along the shore and into the hills. There were maybe five hundred people following him, and the numbers seemed to be ever growing.

Even though we had been moving for some time, I could still see waves of people pushing and shouting, desperately trying to get closer to Yeshua.

It is why we just ended up continually on the move.

It was the only way to avoid being crushed.

Hence why life on the road with Yeshua could be so exhausting.

As we ventured even further along the coast on that second day, Yeshua was talking to those around him, like he always did. But this time, there were so many people and so much chaos that many were struggling to hear him.

I persuaded Yeshua that we should leave the crowds for a moment or two.

To get away. To regroup.

Maybe even recoup.

After all, we hadn't eaten much for the two days we had been out, and I was ravenous.

When we finally managed to leave the crowds behind, Yeshua seemed quietly grateful. The sheer weight of people all day, every day, must have been so draining for him. Yet he never complained. He seemed to love just being among them all.

But on this day, he was happy to have a few moments away, just with us.

'Let's go somewhere quiet,' he said.

That was a welcome comment, trust me.

I was already planning our escape, and it firmly included a fire, and some fish and wine.

We found a small boat and asked the skipper to head around to a patch of hillside without any houses nearby.

It was a good plan that would have worked, if people hadn't seen us climb into the boat. Somehow, the crowd figured out where we were going, because as soon as we rounded the corner of the last cove, and saw where we planned to put ashore, there seemed to be an even bigger crowd of people waiting and shouting out to Yeshua.

And when I say bigger, I don't mean just hundreds of people, but now thousands.

I couldn't believe it. Word must have travelled fast.

My instinct?

I wanted to turn the boat around and find somewhere else. But before any of us could do anything, Yeshua had jumped into the water up to his waist, waded onto the shoreline and started talking to people, putting his hands upon them.

He was back among them as always.

Soon, it was starting to get late and some of us were getting hungry. But the crowds showed no sign of thinning out.

I made my way over to where Yeshua was and quietly suggested that he might want to think about wrapping everything up so that people could get off, get home and get supper.

He looked out at the crowd, now of many thousands. At least four. Maybe five thousand. There were people as far as I could see.

Yeshua looked back at me and fixed me with a gaze that was half mischief and half challenge.

'You do it,' he said. 'Fix supper for them.'

At first, I thought he was joking.

Fix supper for them? How am I going to do that?

But Yeshua wasn't joking. He was just sitting there on a rock, looking at me, like we were back in Kfar Nahum and he'd just asked me to fix a snack for the two of us.

I wasn't sure what he was meaning or whether I had missed something. The others were now looking at me too. Even my brother Andreas looked confused.

'So how am I going to do that?' I blurted out. I was annoyed at Yeshua's frivolity, and I was never great with having everyone looking at me.

Eventually, Yeshua spoke. 'How many loaves of bread do you have?'

A quick estimate from wandering around the crowds and asking a few pertinent questions, and it was soon obvious the answer was: limited supplies all round.

Andreas was the only one of us who had much luck, returning with this shrimpy little kid who was holding out a bag of goods he had been selling.

'He's only got five loaves of barley bread and two little fish left,' Andreas grumbled, making the point about the futility of this whole endeavour.

Yeshua stepped towards the young boy and put his hand

on his shoulder. Then he told us to make everyone in the crowd sit down.

It took a few moments, but eventually I got them to settle. My fisherman's lungs have a good use sometimes.

45

Bread of Life

WHAT HAPPENED NEXT still defies logic.

Yeshua took the little boy's food, prayed and broke the loaves.

Then he divided the food and put it back into the satchel, along with a few baskets we had lying around. Then he told us to start handing the bread and the fish out to all the people.

I can't tell you how it happened because I still don't really understand. But what I do know is that every time I put my hand in one of the baskets to grab either fish or bread there was food waiting for me.

No matter how many people I gave food to, the supply just kept coming.

As we moved around the crowd, the most amazing silence settled on everyone. Nobody spoke. Not even the little kids. People were sitting, waiting with their eyes wide and hands held open waiting to be fed.

I couldn't believe it. The food just kept coming.

When everyone was settled and we had handed out all the food to everyone, Yeshua stood and spoke to them. In words true and clear.

'Do not work for food that does not last,' he told us. 'Work for food that lasts forever.' He paused. 'The Son of Man will give you that kind of food.'

Yeshua continued, his words calm, steady and measured.

'I am the bread of life. He who comes to me will never be hungry. He who puts his trust in me will never be thirsty.' Yeshua let those words sink in, like the bread and fish in all our mouths.

'I will never turn away anyone who comes to me. I came down from heaven. I did not come to do what I wanted to do.

I came to do what my Father wanted me to do. He is the one who sent me.'

He made the point once more: 'The Father sent me. He did not want me to lose any of all those he gave me. He wants me to raise them to life on the last day.'

Then he wrapped it up with this simple statement of intent:

'He wants everyone who sees the Son to put his trust in him and have life that lasts forever. I will raise that one up on the last day.'

And at this, the crowd started to eat, to feast, then soon they began to dance.

By the time all the five thousand people had finished and were starting to make their way back to the surrounding villages, we were high on the moment.

Everyone was.

Yeshua then asked us to go and collect up the leftovers.

When we had finished, there was so much bread and fish left over that we filled twelve massive baskets.

Typical Yeshua. Giving away far more than is ever asked for.

I don't know much about history, but some said it reminded them about Moses and the way God fed the Israelites out in the desert. They were hungry too. God knew that they didn't just need someone to tell them about what their future was going to be like, they needed to fill their bellies today. And God had met their needs beautifully.

Just like this crowd had experienced.

That day, out among the hills overlooking the lake, Yeshua and all of us had feasted like kings.

On the bread of heaven.

46

Ghost

BY THE TIME the crowds had departed, it was dark.

Yeshua sent us ahead as well, telling us to go back to the boat and sail over to the other side of the lake. He said that he wanted to stay back alone to pray.

I know he loved his times of solitude after being with so many people, but it didn't make sense to me, to send us out onto the waters in the dark when we could stay and wait for him on shore.

But Yeshua insisted, and said he would meet us on the far shore.

I still thought he was mad. What was the point of sending us away by boat and then having to walk all the way around to join us?

And anyway, how could we protect him from any further crowds, or even bandits by night, if he sent us away?

I wanted to say something, but after having questioned his feeding plans earlier, I decided not to second-guess him this time, so I kept my mouth shut. Instead, I left Yeshua as asked and followed the rest of the crew back to the boat.

We then pushed off in silence.

For a while, nothing much happened. It was dark already when we put out onto the water, but it was a clear night with a good moon, so it was easy enough to make headway towards the other side of the lake.

Soon, a few of the others started drifting off to sleep.

I stayed awake and helmed the boat, with the north star as my guide.

We'd just reached about halfway when the wind picked up. It was blowing us strongly towards our destination. The waves and wind increased and soon I made the call to drop anchor.

It would be suicidal to try to come ashore in these breaking waves and strong onshore winds. We'd destroy the boat – and probably ourselves.

Sometimes, as a fisherman, you must know when to hold off and sit out gale force conditions. Even if it means a long, wet night ahead.

I reckoned the storm would blow through in a few hours and we could then land at dawn.

We dropped anchor a mile out, divided the night into watches and hoped the wind would die down soon.

None of us slept and we were all soaking wet. Some of the non-fishermen among us were terrified, but I was fine. It wasn't the first time I'd had to wait out a squall – not by a long shot.

I curled into the bottom of the boat and tried to rest.

I remembered the other time we had gone out on the lake with Yeshua, and we got caught up in that massive storm. That one had been different. It really could have taken us all down to our graves.

Back then, Yeshua had made the storm disappear with one command. It had been mind-blowing to see.

We were all dog tired, and I was beginning to wish we had him with us now.

Not long before first light, the wind was dying down a little. I was on watch and trying not to doze off. I remember looking east, hoping for the first rays of the dawn ahead.

Just then, I heard one of the others scream.

I still don't know who said it, but I remember the word like it was yesterday.

'Ghost!'

47

Walking on Water

EVERYONE ON THE boat was staring into the black, just off the port bow, their eyes pinned wide with terror. They were shaking, shouting over and over that there was some sort of ghost out there.

I looked intently.

I doubted them. They were tired, that's all. It happens often. The mariner's mirage.

The clouds had rolled in as well, so visibility was low now. At first, I saw nothing. Just the waves closest to the boat. Beyond it was nothing but darkness.

I told them to forget it.

Then suddenly, Yakov shouted, 'Look! Over there! It's coming towards us!'

I scanned again. Then I saw it.

There was something out there. A shadow. Like a person.

I wasn't sure at first, but the more I stared, the clearer it became. Something was out there in the darkness. Walking straight towards us across the waves.

The figure was walking on the water.

Soon everyone was yelling and screaming – including me, I admit. It's not exactly something you ever prepare yourself for seeing.

We were all scared to death as this mysterious figure continued silently right towards us.

I had always been a superstitious man, just like my father too. Fishermen often are. And what I was seeing in front of me was truly terrifying.

I was about ready to dive into the water and take my chance in there, rather than face this spirit – or whatever it was in front of us.

I was ready to go.

But then the figure spoke. And I suddenly realised who it was.

It was Yeshua. Walking, floating above the waves. Like an apparition.

In all my life, I had never felt so relieved and yet so in awe at the same time.

And with Yeshua, I'd seen some incredible things. Trust me.

Then Yeshua spoke to us. 'Courage. It's me. Don't be afraid.'

To be honest, I wasn't sure what I was thinking. I still thought maybe I was seeing things. I mean, humans don't walk on water.

Then on instinct, I called out to him, 'If it's really you, call me to come to you on the water!' It was a foolish thing to say in the heat of the moment.

'Come on,' Yeshua said, without missing a beat.

I looked around at the others, all cowering in the stern together.

'Come on,' he repeated.

Like I said, I'm impulsive. So, without any further thought, I jumped out of the boat, landed on top of the waves, and somehow, I didn't sink.

I couldn't believe it.

I tentatively started making my way over towards Yeshua. Across the water. It was the most incredible feeling.

At first, I wasn't really thinking about the fact that I was actually walking on water. I was just thinking about how I wanted to get to Yeshua.

I think subconsciously I felt that would be the safest place to be.

Then at that point, I made a fatal error.

I looked down.

Down at the waves beneath.

And I started to panic. Then I started to sink.

'Master!' I yelled, feeling myself sinking deeper and deeper down. 'Help me!'

Yeshua didn't move to start with. He was willing me on and reaching out his hand.

But I was sinking – and fast.

Then Yeshua walked to me, reached out, grabbed my hand and lifted me up.

'What got into you?' he said, his voice full of warmth but with a hint of teasing.

I couldn't speak. And I certainly was not going to start a dialogue with him right now.

'Just get me to the boat!' I shouted.

I let Yeshua guide me back to the boat – still walking on water – and then I collapsed back on board.

As soon as Yeshua and I were back in the boat, everyone was overawed with excitement.

'It is true . . . You are God's Son indeed!'

As for me? I had already figured that part out in my head and heart. Even though I might not have said it.

But right then, I was too busy shaking to join in their excitement. My old bones were still rattling out of fear and relief, and I was the coldest I'd ever been in my life.

But something had happened between Yeshua and me out on that lake, I just didn't understand what.

I now know it's what he would describe as 'faith'. But unless you've ever taken that step into the great unknown, it is impossible to explain.

48

How to Pray

AFTER WHAT HAPPENED out on the lake, I wanted to be with Yeshua all the time. I was in. Where he was going, I would go too.

I knew goodness and truth when I saw it. And he was it.

Being with Yeshua always felt like the most radical place to be. And it was most certainly never boring. I learnt to expect the unexpected – every day. I loved that. He brought real life to everything, and he transformed people's lives – no surprises there, I suppose. After all, he had told us on that hillside: he was the 'bread of life'.

Being so close to Yeshua was, at times, a dangerous place to be.

But as a fisherman I was no stranger to danger and fear.

The crowds were still following us around daily, and ever since Yohanan's death, Yeshua had been spending more and more time alone. Early morning before people came, or late in the evening when they'd gone, he'd walk up some hillside or other and disappear for an hour or so alone.

He would often sit there, eyes closed, head raised, and just be smiling. Like he was somehow getting power into him from above. I envied that so much. I wanted to be able to do it too.

Which was why one day, just when he was about to head off on his own again, I asked him, 'Can you teach me how to refresh like you do – with God? Is it really possible? How do I do it?'

Like everyone, I'd grown up with the words of a few trad-itional prayers and psalms. But they sometimes felt distant and formulaic to me. I wasn't sure that they would ever really help me.

Yeshua looked at me, smiled, then reached out and held my hands in his.

The few others gathered with us had now stopped what they were doing, and they were watching for his response. Yeshua told us all to sit down with him.

We sat silent – waiting. We wanted to know how Yeshua spoke with the Lord God himself. The Mighty One. The One who spoke to Moses from a burning bush, and who led the escaping Israelites with clouds by day and fire by night.

Yeshua leaned forward, inviting us to do the same.

'Don't bargain with God. Be direct. Ask for what you need.'

He smiled at us.

'This is not a cat-and-mouse, hide-and-seek game we're in. If your little boy asks for a serving of fish, do you scare him with a live snake on his plate? If your little girl asks for an egg, do you trick her with a spider? As bad as you are,' he said, winking at us, 'you wouldn't think of such a thing – you're at least decent to your own children.'

That was true, I thought.

He continued. 'How much more will your Father in heaven give the Holy Spirit to those who ask him.'

He paused.

'How much more.'

Then he continued. 'When you pray,' his voice was quiet now, 'say: "Father, reveal who you are. Set the world right."'

He paused again.

'Keep us alive with three square meals. Keep us forgiven with you and forgiving others. Keep us safe from ourselves and the devil.'

And then he stopped. That was it.

It felt like he wasn't only teaching us what to pray, but *how* to pray.

I liked that. *Keep it simple. Keep it honest.*

Some of what he said was surprising to me though.

Was he saying we could call God our Father? Really?

That wasn't what I'd been taught traditionally.

I had always been instructed that even the name of God wasn't to be spoken out loud, in reverence. And here was Yeshua telling us to call him like our closest relative or friend.

It was bold.

But that's what he said.

Yeshua, God's own Son, here in flesh and blood, sitting with us, and saying that it was possible for us to call Almighty God our Father. No grovelling, no hiding and no fear.

And then the fact that Yeshua said we could ask God for things. That was new. We could call out to him, like we were his children, and he was our dad. That was radical.

Was it possible to speak to God like this? Could we really ask him for stuff, in the way Yeshua was saying?

But that's what he had said, so I went with it.

Why wouldn't I?

All I had to do was speak my heart, give my heart and ask for help.

That night, I just sat there on my own, thinking about it all. I tried to pray like this.

It felt simple, natural, unreligious and uncomplicated.

Kind of like Yeshua himself.

Then I lay there, trying to work out what it was that I wanted to ask my Father in heaven for.

There was a lot to choose from.

But annoyingly, I fell asleep midway through.

49

Believe in Me

NOT ALL YESHUA'S teaching was so simple to follow. And at times it got intense.

'Don't run from suffering; embrace it,' he once told us.

And, 'You cannot serve God and money.' That was another.

Some of the group left at that point. They did not want to follow such hard teaching any longer.

Money often seems to be a great divider.

Then the time Yeshua told us all, 'If anyone would come after me, let him deny himself and take up his cross daily and follow me.'

It was interesting how so many turned away from tough talk like this.

Or the time when he told everyone in the temple that they were slaves.

'The truth will set you free,' he said.

That didn't go down well with the Pharisees.

'We're Abraham's descendants, and we have never been slaves. So why do you say that we will be free?'

Yeshua didn't hold back.

'Everyone who sins is a slave – a slave to sin,' he replied.

Then he went even further.

'I know you are Abraham's descendants, but you want to kill me because you don't want to accept my teaching. I am telling you what my Father has shown me.'

They started murmuring at this. It was blasphemous talk.

'My Father, whom you claim as your God, is the one who glorifies me. Though you do not know him, I know him.'

Then Yeshua dropped his head and closed his eyes, as if tired of explaining himself. Over and over. To deaf ears.

In a low voice, he then spoke. 'Your father Abraham rejoiced at the thought of seeing my day; he saw it and was glad.'

At this they laughed at him.

'You are not yet fifty years old,' they said, 'and you have seen Abraham?'

Yeshua paused, and slowly everyone fell silent.

'Truly I tell you,' Yeshua replied, 'before Abraham was born, I am!'

Those words. 'I am.'

The very words used by our forefathers to describe the Almighty himself. It was too much. And they started picking up stones to throw at him.

But Yeshua, and those of us with him, quickly slipped away.

There were many moments like this, and they just made me all the more determined to stay – after all, I have never been a quitter.

I remember once, Yeshua told those of us who had stuck with him a simple truth: 'For whoever would save his life will lose it, but whoever loses his life for my sake will save it. For what does it profit a man if he gains the whole world and loses or forfeits himself?'

Those words have always stayed with me.

For other followers, it was too much when he started talking about who was in charge if they wanted to follow him.

'Anyone who intends to come with me has to let me lead. You're not in the driver's seat – I am. Follow me and I'll show you how. Self-help is no help at all. Self-sacrifice is the way, my way, to finding yourself, your true self. What good would it do to get everything you want and lose you, the real you?'

'Does this rattle you?' he asked the remaining twelve of us one day, after a few more people had left. 'Do you also want to leave?'

I didn't wait to see what the others were thinking.

I was operating on impulse, so I replied boldly, 'Master, to whom would we go? You have the words of real life, eternal life. We've already committed ourselves, confident that you are the Holy One of God.'

He looked at me with a warmth that is hard to describe.

It was a good moment. A great moment.

Yeshua then reached left and right, putting his hands on those who flanked him.

'I'm telling you the most solemn and sober truth now: whoever believes in me has real life, eternal life.' Yeshua paused, 'Whoever is thirsty may come to me and drink. Rivers of living water will flow out from their heart. This is what the Scriptures say.'

And I believed. I had seen too much to deny it.

50

Who Am I?

THAT FEELING OF being in time and tune with Yeshua got stronger by the day.

It felt so natural. When I stopped fighting, stopped trying to lead, stopped over thinking, and simply surrendered to his way – to his way of revolutionary love – life fell into rhythm and place.

While we were in Kfar Nahum, those of us closest to Yeshua stayed in my house. It was good to see Yeshua laughing, joking and relaxing a bit. Ever since he'd healed my mother-in-law, way back when Andreas and I had first started following him, he had become her favourite adopted son.

There was nothing she wouldn't do for him. And we teased him mercilessly about it.

One day, when we were on the road together, heading North, Yeshua asked us plainly, 'What are people saying about who the Son of Man is?'

I don't know who replied first, but someone said people had different ideas about him – some thinking he was Yohanan the Baptiser, or Elijah, Jeremiah or one of the other prophets come back to life.

'And how about you?' he asked us. 'Who do you say I am?'

There was a heavy silence. I waited for someone else to speak, but nobody did. They all just sat there, looking a bit sheepish, a bit awkward.

As if unsure of how to say it.

I couldn't stand it. *'Just say it straight,'* I thought. *'Stop being cowards.'*

So, I stood up and spoke aloud the words that we'd all whispered to each other a hundred times already.

'You're the Christ, the Messiah, the Son of the living God.'

The silence felt like it lasted a year.

Yeshua sat perfectly still, his expression neutral as he stared at me.

And then it broke, and a massive smile spread across his face.

'God bless you,' he laughed. 'You didn't get that answer out of books or from teachers. My Father in heaven, God himself, let you in on this secret of who I really am. And now I'm going to tell you who you are, really are.'

He paused for effect.

It worked. I held my breath and waited.

'You are Kephas, which means 'rock', and on this rock I will build my community, and the gates of hell will not overcome it.'

My cheeks were burning up, and I didn't know where to put my hands, but I was happy. That was quite a moment.

Yeshua wasn't done yet, either.

'And that's not all,' he said, still speaking just to me. 'You will have complete and free access to God's kingdom, keys to open any and every door: no more barriers between heaven and earth, earth and heaven.'

I felt overwhelmed to be honest. Head spinning. These words of Yeshua would sustain me through so much in the coming months and years.

But ahead were also some moments of true shame for me. I am just thankful I did not know it at this time. I don't think I would have been able to bear the knowledge of my failings to come.

Yeshua soon started talking about the plan for what was going to happen next.

He said that he had to go to Yerushalayim, and that when he got there, he'd suffer greatly, at the hands of the religious leaders.

I listened carefully. I'd heard him talk about suffering before. But what Yeshua was saying troubled me. He was the Son of God, so how come the religious leaders could have any kind of authority over him? Let alone be able to hurt him?

After all, he could walk on water and turn the stuff into wine.

But before I could even bring this up with him, he became more explicit. And the mood turned fast.

Yeshua said that he was going to be killed.

But that on the third day he would be raised up alive again.

Nobody uttered a sound.

But Yeshua seemed fine.

He stood up and walked on, as if the plans he'd just shared were about what we might eat that night or where we might stay on the way down to the city.

I didn't know what to think. I just felt sick.

As he wandered away, I felt the same feeling I'd had on the boat. The same feeling I'd had earlier when I'd told him I thought he was the Messiah. Pure and simple. And I knew exactly what I needed to do now.

After all, hadn't he just said that I was the rock on which he would build his future community and church? This was my cue to speak up.

I caught up with him, took hold of his arm to stop him in his tracks. 'Master,' I said, 'I won't let all this happen. It cannot be!'

Yeshua turned and didn't miss a beat.

He looked right at me and barked, 'Satan, get out of my way.' He was breathing heavily and looked full of fury and nerves.

Then he calmed down and dropped his head. He placed his hand on my shoulder and looked me in the eye.

'You have no idea how God works.'

I felt my knees buckle beneath me and I grabbed on tight to his hands.

Then I felt my heart break.

51

Dead Men Talking

I DON'T THINK I'd ever really known what shame was before that day.

In fact, I had never been a good one for admitting I was wrong in life.

It just wasn't how I'd been raised.

Our family always tended to be right. Or so we thought.

But as I felt his words explode again and again inside me, I felt the life being squeezed out of me. I felt like I was drowning in shame.

When all was right between Yeshua and me, I felt unconquerable. But when I felt any distance from him, my courage and strength seemed to leave me.

It was a lesson I would learn again and again, often only too painfully.

In the days that followed, I felt more and more like a leaking boat. I was like some kind of 25-footer with a huge hole right on the waterline. I was sinking.

I could feel it in my bones.

And then, just when I thought that maybe I should pack up and join the dozens of ex-followers who had turned their backs on Yeshua, he announced that we were going on another trip. And he only wanted Yakov, Yohanan and me to go with him.

Only a few days earlier, it seemed Yeshua couldn't decide if I was the rock on which he was building his church or Satan himself.

I wasn't sure what was going on. But I wasn't going to say no. I just followed Yeshua, Yakov and Yohanan as they headed out towards the mountains.

And I kept my questions to myself.

If you ask me, there are two types of people in this world.

There are sea people and there are mountain people.

You're either one or the other.

I'm a water man. The further away from a boat I get, the more unsettled I feel. And if you take me to the base of a mountain so high that you can't see the top, and then tell me that we're going to climb all the way up, I'm going to struggle not to start swearing and telling you that mountains are for goats.

And Yeshua didn't just pick any mountain.

He picked one of the biggest ones I'd ever seen.

The rockiest, steepest, cloudiest peak in the region, and as we stood at the bottom and stared up – me having to lean all the way back to be able to see the top – I was convinced that this was either his way of punishing me or forcing me to quit.

But I told you I'm not a quitter. So, I got my head down and started walking.

It was tough going from the get-go. Soon my legs were on fire and my chest felt like it was going to explode. I was cursing in my head, and more than once the curses came out loud.

I was covered in sweat and had to stop every few paces to get my breath back. Yakov and Yohanan were skinnier than me, but even they were struggling a bit. And all the time, Yeshua was pushing on ahead, picking his way up the rocks like there was some kind of treasure waiting for him at the top.

Little did I know what we were heading up to.

When finally Yakov, Yohanan and I scrambled up the last rocky outcrop, we flopped down onto our backs at the top.

Then we saw Yeshua.

He was standing just ahead of us, side on, looking like I'd never seen him before.

Everything about him was changing, right before our eyes. Sunlight was pouring from his face. His clothes were filled with this brilliant light. It was somehow inside of him, as if he had swallowed the sun itself.

It was incredible. Beautiful. I forgot all my sweat, pain and fatigue and just stared, eyes wide open.

'Look! Look!' stammered Yohanan, now pointing either side of Yeshua.

I hadn't seen it at first – I'd been too taken with this amazing transformation that was happening in the Master. But as I looked, I saw that Yeshua wasn't alone. There were two other people with him.

Men dressed like wild desert nomads. And the three of them were talking.

All of them were bathed in the amazing light that was coming out of Yeshua.

We just sat frozen, staring at the three of them.

We couldn't hear what they were saying, but the more we stared, the more we wondered out loud.

Isn't that . . .?

Can it really be . . .?

Because as far as I was concerned, the two men he was talking to had been dead for centuries.

52

Listen

I DON'T KNOW why, but the fact that I was watching Yeshua emblazoned with light, talking to Moses and Elijah, somehow didn't surprise me.

I guess with Yeshua I had become acclimatised to expecting the unexpected. After all, it wasn't so long ago that I had walked alongside him on the water.

That's not something you can say every day.

So, there we were.

Yohanan and Yakov had now thrown themselves on the ground, calling out prayers of thanks and praise. But not me. I was just trying to work it all out.

Now, I'm no scholar, but I knew enough about Moses and Elijah to understand they had both helped to lead and to guide God's people. Moses was the giver of the law, and Elijah was the great prophet.

Arguably, neither of them had completed their tasks.

Moses hadn't made it to the Promised Land, and the people continued to rebel after Elijah's time on earth was over. But they had given everything and pointed the way.

It is just that someone else was going to have to finish the job.

It was obvious.

Yeshua had told us repeatedly.

He was going to fulfil all those promises that Elijah and Moses, and the rest of the prophets, had talked about.

Yeshua was the one we had all been waiting for.

I started thinking about Moses, and how he'd gone up a mountain too. The old story says that he even saw the glory of the Lord, and Moses' face had shone brightly, reflecting that glory back.

But here was Yeshua, not reflecting God's glory, but transmitting it. The light was shining out of him like he was the sun itself.

The light of the world.

Suddenly, I felt the old familiar urge to say or do something. That impulse again. I wanted to make sure that this moment was never forgotten.

The words rushed up from deep inside me, and nothing I could do would keep them down.

'Yeshua, this is amazing!' I screamed.

Yakov and Yohanan were still face down, but Yeshua looked over. It was only a glance. But it was all I needed.

I started jumping up and down, so full of awe and adrenalin I thought I was going to burst.

'Master! What would you think if I built three memorials here on the mountain – one for you, one for Moses, one for Elijah?'

And then the voice stopped me in my tracks, and I buckled to the ground.

This massive voice started thundering out of the mountain itself.

'This is my Son, marked by my love, focus of my delight.'

I had always known the story about what happened to Yeshua when Yohanan the Baptiser took him down into the Yarden river. When God's voice had boomed out of the sky, telling everyone that Yeshua was his Son.

I knew all that, but I never dreamt that I'd hear it for myself.

The voice came again. And I knew, without doubt, that it was the Lord God Almighty.

The words were booming – crystal clear and loud.

'Listen to him.'

53

Not a Word

IT WAS MY turn to throw myself down on the ground beside Yakov and Yohanan. I was terrified, partly because God himself had just given me a verbal slap for being a fool, but mainly because of what I had just heard booming out of the sky.

There was such power in God's voice that I suddenly felt weaker than I'd ever felt at any point in my life. It wasn't that God's words were loud. It was because they were true.

God was right there, closer than the air in my lungs and the dirt against my skin. God was there. Here.

Then I felt a hand on my shoulder. I lifted my head and opened my eyes.

'Don't be afraid,' said Yeshua. He was crouched down in front of me, looking right into my eyes. And he was smiling.

I sat up and looked around.

Moses and Elijah were gone, but I didn't want to ask where to or what they'd been talking about. I didn't want to say anything, given the trouble my big mouth had got me into before.

I just did what Yakov and Yohanan did and followed Yeshua as he began the long walk back down the mountain.

None of us spoke until we were almost at the bottom.

Yeshua paused and turned to us. His face intense.

'Don't breathe a word of what you've seen,' he said.

I nodded. As far as I was concerned, I was done with talking altogether.

Yeshua turned to start walking, but after a few steps he paused again and looked back at us. He stared each of us in the eye and simply added:

'After I'm raised from the dead, you are free to talk.'

54

Have Mercy

I COULDN'T PUT it out of my mind.

Yeshua had told us, plain as day, that he was going to be handed over and killed, but that he would then come back to life.

It was the first part that troubled me most.

If Yeshua was going to suffer and be killed, I wasn't sure I could bear seeing it. And why would it happen? He was perfect. And kind.

Always loving, affirming and inclusive to everyone.

It broke my heart just to hear of it.

But my gut told me that he was speaking the truth. Yeshua always did.

He had spoken of all this before. But there was a renewed intensity now.

Months earlier, when we were celebrating Hanukkah in Yerushalayim, the Master told a story about a shepherd and his sheep. He said that the sheep will follow their master, who they know, but they won't follow a stranger.

We didn't really understand what he was saying, so he spelled it out.

'A thief comes to steal, kill and destroy. But I came to give life – life that is full and good. I am the good shepherd, and the good shepherd gives his life for his sheep.'

I have never forgotten those end words.

But it didn't stop there. A few days later, we were walking through Solomon's colonnade in the temple, when someone spotted Yeshua and the crowds began to surge around him. This time, many more of the officials were there and they looked menacing.

'How long are you going to keep us guessing?' they asked. 'If you're the Messiah, tell us straight out.'

Yeshua held their gaze. Without even blinking he replied, 'I've already told you . . . but you do not believe because you are not my sheep. Everything I have done has been authorised by my Father, actions that speak louder than words . . . I and the Father are one.'

His words landed like a punch, and the situation quickly turned ugly. People were running and shouting. Searching for rocks heavy enough to smash a skull.

Yeshua just stood there, like he owned the place. Bold as a lion.

'I have shown you many good works from the Father,' he said, 'For which of these do you stone me?'

That stalled them for a moment.

Then one of the Pharisees replied, 'We're going to stone you, not because of what you've done but what you've just said.'

A silence temporarily descended in the crowd.

'You, a mere man, claiming to be God!'

Then someone yelled 'Blasphemer' and all hell broke loose.

I still don't know how we got Yeshua out of there alive. It was a moment of raw fear for me. A small taste of what lay ahead . . .

Soon after we got back from the mountain and were reunited with the rest of our little group, Yeshua called everyone together and told them the same message: how he was going to be killed but would come back to life. But he was even more explicit now.

'The Son of Man is about to be betrayed to some people who want nothing to do with God. They will murder him.' Yeshua paused. Then smiled and reached out to touch us. 'Three days later he will be raised alive.'

Yeshua held nothing back. We would be heading to Yerushalayim, and the worst was about to happen.

Almost as soon as he'd explained all this, we were off again. As was always his way.

We left Galilee behind us and headed south.

I felt that Yeshua was different after that time up the mountain. He was even more focused and single-minded. He had an intensity about him that was disconcerting.

It made me nervous.

Back in the early days, we'd always ambled down to Yerushalayim, stopping at every place we found to drink goat's milk and honey, and sometimes wine. We would laugh more than was deemed normal, rib each other ruthlessly, sleep in the shade under olive trees, play pranks, splash in rivers, and he still seemed to have time to change people's lives along the way.

But now we moved like the wind.

We barely stopped for breath, and we walked as fast and for as long as we could. Yeshua wasn't saying much either, but when he did it felt like he only wanted to talk about what lay ahead.

My heart broke every time he did this. I didn't know what I could do to change anything.

We got to Yericho quicker than I expected. There was still enough light left in the day and Yeshua wanted to press on for Yerushalayim.

So, we did.

When we passed by the outskirts of Yericho, a beggar called out to Yeshua, 'Master! Have mercy on me!'

Those of us that were closest to the man told him to be quiet and move out the way. In hindsight, it wasn't our finest moment, I admit.

And of course, what happened? First, Yeshua stops.

Then he said to bring the man over.

The beggar was blind, and when someone had helped him over, Yeshua asked him what he wanted.

'Master,' he said. 'I want to see again.'

And of course, Yeshua responded.

'Go ahead – see again!' he said. 'Your faith has saved and healed you.'

And just like that, the man could suddenly see. His eyelids opened, and light filled his vision. He could see everything in full colour.

A smile spread across his face that was like the sun rising

on a beautiful spring day. The man then started laughing and weeping and hugging Yeshua.

He would not let Yeshua go. He was indeed a man reborn.

It reminded me of those early days when we'd wander around Galilee and all the sick people would flock to Yeshua for help.

And of course, he always obliged.

Healing. Restoring.

55

Hearts Made New

WHILE WE WERE in Yericho, I'd noticed this guy, short as anything, with ratty, beady eyes, following us. Always at a distance. He was no beggar. He was dressed more like royalty. Although he wasn't, because people avoided being near him – like a leper. But he wasn't that either.

I couldn't quite figure him out, but I didn't trust him.

Instinct.

The little guy was trying to stay out of the way of the crowds, yet at the same time he seemed desperate to get a proper view of Yeshua.

He was obviously after something.

I lost him in the crowd at one point, but eventually spotted him climbing a tree and poking his head out of the branches.

He looked ridiculous.

Then I clocked what he was.

It was the way that those around him shunned him with a furtive look of disdain. He was a tax collector. Clear and simple. They are always among the most despised and corrupt people you'll come across.

I'd wager this rat would sell his own grandmother to feather his own nest and protect his insider dealings with the Romans.

If any soul was rotten, it was corrupt tax collectors.

When Yeshua got close to the tree that the man was hiding in, he stopped. Yeshua looked up and stared right at him.

'Zacchaeus,' he announced, like he'd been expecting him all along. 'Hurry down. Today is my day to be a guest in your home.'

The tax collector looked stunned for a second, then pointed at himself.

'What? Me?'

Then a massive grin spread across his face as he scrambled down and hurriedly started to lead Yeshua to his home.

Yeshua followed without a care in the world.

I was surprised.

It's one thing hanging out with the poor and sick. But to be associated with the corrupt and traitorous? That was something else.

I wasn't certain how wise a move this was.

The whole crowd started to follow them both. You could sense the whispered murmurings.

Why would Yeshua show such honour and respect to a scumbag like Zacchaeus?

Did Yeshua realise who he was?

I was still holding back, observing and saying nothing, although part of me sympathised with the crowd. I had always despised tax collectors too.

Someone like Zacchaeus was obviously bringing all kinds of misery to the good people of Yericho. Why encourage him?

When we got to his home, I was amazed. I'd never been in a house like it. The whole place was like a gilded palace, draped with exotic tapestries, refined opulence, good wine and ample servants.

And yet there was Yeshua, calmly standing in the middle of the home, being welcomed by Zacchaeus.

But then something happened.

I couldn't hear their conversation. Yeshua had his hand on Zacchaeus as he often did with people before something would change.

Zacchaeus was looking at Yeshua, then looking around at all his wealth. I noticed he had tears in his eyes. Then he held Yeshua's hand and dropped to his knees. His chest was heaving with emotion now, his rich cloak fell from his shoulders, and he looked like a small boy before Yeshua.

'Master!' he sobbed. 'My Lord!'

Yeshua had that look about him, like he'd known all along this was going to happen.

It took Zacchaeus ages to get his breath back and finally be able to string a sentence together. But instantly I could see something was different.

'Master, I'm giving away half my income to the poor – and if I've cheated anyone, I'm paying four times the damages.'

Then at once, Zacchaeus opened his purse and started handing out coins right there, right then. He invited anyone from outside to come in. He embraced them, he promised to make good on those he had wronged, and he instructed his servants to take ledgers and notes for any repayments he owed.

But above all, his face had changed.

It shone. His eyes were bright, and his heart and hands were open.

I couldn't quite believe it to be honest.

Yeshua just looked on, a look of pride in his eyes, and spoke in a warm voice: 'Today is salvation day, in this home.'

At this, everyone cheered.

Zacchaeus called for the wine servers to open the doors and serve everyone. The music started and the most beautiful of street parties began. Everyone in the town got involved.

I'd seen many physical miracles with Yeshua, but in some ways, when you see rotten hearts made new, it was just as beautiful and powerful.

To this day, I don't know what Yeshua said to the man to change him – Yeshua never actually told us – but maybe sometimes it isn't words. Yeshua simply saw the beautiful and the good that was inside of Zacchaeus. And he let it out.

When I asked Yeshua about why he picked out Zacchaeus at the beginning, he had simply told me, 'The Son of Man came to seek and to save the lost.'

By the time we left Zacchaeus' house, the streets were full of people shouting and cheering. Many were weeping and laughing as Yeshua passed by.

Within days, such an atmosphere would be totally eclipsed.

Soon, the laughter would end.

56

Come Out

THE NEXT DAY, Yeshua got a message from his friends Myriam and Marta.

Their brother, Elazar, was sick.

Yeshua and Elazar had long been close friends – almost as close as he'd been to his cousin Yohanan. So, when I heard the news of his illness, I assumed we'd head off right away.

Again, I was wrong.

Yeshua said that we would wait. We would stay put a little longer.

'This sickness will not end in death,' he told us.

But still, knowing that Elazar was sick bothered me. I had a bad feeling about it. Yet I kept my mouth shut. No more gaffes.

Finally, after three days, Yeshua announced that the time was right to go to see Elazar, Myriam and Marta.

Yeshua told us that Elazar had fallen asleep, and that he was going to wake him up.

I didn't understand what he was talking about.

All he said was that we were about to be given 'new grounds for believing'.

It took most of the day to make it up to Beth 'Anya. The walk itself was hot and the sun was brutal as we trudged up the steep trails.

By the time we arrived, we were all sweating and exhausted.

Marta ran out to us and met Yeshua before we'd even reached the house. She was dressed in black, and the pair talked quietly. She was crying.

Her brother had been dead for four days, she told us.

Then she looked at Yeshua and whispered, 'He wouldn't have died if you had been here.'

Yeshua held her in his arms.

Marta continued, 'But I know that even now God will give you whatever you ask.'

She was distraught and all our hearts broke for her.

I felt confused.

Yeshua had promised us that this would not happen. But we had delayed and now it was too late.

Yeshua held her head in his chest as she sobbed.

Then he whispered to her, 'Your brother will rise again.'

'I know,' she replied through her tears. 'One day. At the end of time.'

Yeshua leaned in. 'You don't have to wait for the end,' he said, his eyes now locked on her. 'Everyone who lives believing in me does not ultimately die at all. Do you believe this?'

'Yes, Master,' she replied. The words came out in a broken stammer. 'All along I have believed that you are the Messiah, the Son of God who comes into the world.'

Myriam was now with them. Also distraught with anguish.

Yeshua's eyes filled with tears, and he asked to be shown where Elazar was buried.

They led him over to the tomb.

I didn't know what to think.

Part of me had just assumed that Elazar was going to be all right when Yeshua arrived at Beth 'Anya. But now, standing in front of a sealed-up tomb, watching tears roll down Yeshua's cheeks, my worst fears were confirmed.

What could Yeshua possibly do for a person who was four days dead?

There were others now gathered around us, and I heard one person ask in a whispered tone, 'If he loved him so much, why didn't he come when Elazar was alive?'

Yeshua then took a step forward towards the tomb. He wiped the tears from his face and placed his hand against the rock.

'Take away the stone,' he announced in a strong voice.

I could sense people's reaction, and it wasn't comfortable.

Marta reminded him discreetly that Elazar had been dead for four days. It was not possible to open it up. The smell of the decomposing corpse would be too strong.

But Yeshua insisted. 'Take away the stone.' He had a wild look in his eyes now. He wasn't just upset, he seemed full of fury. As if he was somehow angry at death itself. He turned to us, his voice loud with emotion: 'Did I not tell you that if you believe, you will see the glory of God?'

Myriam and Marta looked around then nodded to the crowd, and two men hesitatingly stepped forward and started to roll the stone back, so that the tomb was laid bare and open.

Yeshua stood there in front of it. His eyes closed and his head tilted up.

The others backed away – out of respect for the dead.

Then Yeshua spoke loud and clear. 'Father,' he said, his eyes now open and ablaze. 'That they may believe that you sent me.'

Then Yeshua shouted, 'Elazar, come out!'

Nobody moved.

Nobody spoke.

We all just watched the tomb's entrance. But nothing stirred.

Then I heard a noise from within the tomb. And a shadow moved inside.

Then suddenly, Elazar stumbled out of the tomb. Still wrapped in his burial cloth.

He was alive.

Right in front of my very eyes, I saw it. As God is my witness.

Yeshua had just brought Elazar back to life.

57

The Plot

WHAT HAPPENED AT Beth 'Anya changed things.

When word got to the Sanhedrin of a man being raised from the dead, all hell broke loose.

Literally.

Such things must surely be sorcery – or demonic.

A private meeting of the council of priests and Pharisees was called. And their anger was palpable.

As was the fear.

The religious elite might have a reputation for being proud and prudish, but they are not fools.

It was clear that they were alert to the growing influence of this renegade teacher, his so-called miracles, false teaching and blasphemy. And they were also alert to how such a person might threaten the status quo they enjoyed. Not to mention that Yeshua was becoming ever-more popular.

Among the Pharisees and Sadducees was at least one man who wasn't panicking. It was Kaiaphas, the high priest that year. He wasn't like the others. He wasn't content just to sit and fret about what might go wrong.

Kaiaphas was a man of action.

Even if that action included murder.

As they gathered in the synagogue chambers, Kaiaphas knew exactly how to handle this clandestine gathering and this troubling development.

'Can't you see that it's to our advantage that one man dies for the people rather than the whole nation be destroyed?'

Kaiaphas let the words hang in the air. He let the priests and Pharisees slowly absorb what he had just said.

He let them get used to the idea of having Yeshua killed.

How little did he realise the true meaning of his words.
His next question was simpler.
'Now to the "how?"'

58

Celebration

WHEN WE GOT word about the meeting and that there was now a plot to kill Yeshua, I was furious.

The first thing I did was try to persuade Yeshua to head back north, where it was safer.

Despite what Yeshua had said about being killed and rising from the dead, I wasn't going to sit idly by and simply let it happen.

Yeshua did finally agree to move further away from the city. So, we left Beth 'Anya and headed back to the desert and the town of Efraim.

I hoped we could be quiet there. And that this all might simply blow over.

And for a few days it worked.

There was no more teaching in synagogues. No more walking into crowded towns and healing people. No more gathering the masses and feeding them a picnic of miracles.

There was just the twelve of us and Yeshua staying in a small, dusty, barren town where, for once, our reputation hadn't preceded us.

I started to calm down. But Yeshua still seemed tense.

We stayed in a house that was as basic as you can find – four mud walls, a roof and one small door. I didn't quite know what we were to do next.

But Yeshua did.

He told us we were waiting for Passover.

And I knew that Passover was just around the corner.

Within a few days, Yeshua announced we were going to make a short trip back to Beth 'Anya.

We'd heard rumours that the Pharisees had issued orders

for Yeshua to be arrested on sight, and to me, such a journey felt like an unnecessary risk.

But I had long stopped fighting Yeshua.

If he wanted to go, we would go.

We reached Beth 'Anya late in the day and headed straight for the house of Shimon the Leper. It was strange how people still called him that, as ever since Yeshua had healed him, he'd had no sign of leprosy at all. He was one of the healthiest looking people I knew – bright eyes, clear skin. He even had all his teeth, which was rare.

Shimon was back in his family home now, working and able to throw the kind of parties that people flocked to. Tonight was such a time.

His house was full by the time we arrived. The party had been going for hours. And with good reason, because right in the middle of the house, surrounded by people, was Elazar.

A couple of weeks since his miraculous return and people were still flocking to see Elazar. To see the man for themselves, who one moment had been dead, buried and decomposing in a tomb, and four days later, had walked out.

They couldn't get enough of being with him. They kept touching him, asking questions. They wanted to know how he felt, what he remembered and how come he looked so good.

Because just like Shimon the Leper, Elazar's healing had left him stronger and fitter than ever.

Seeing him and Shimon standing next to each other, smiling and laughing, their eyes alert and their voices clear, it was impossible not to be in awe.

When Yeshua walked in, everything kicked off.

Shimon saw him and yelled with delight, and he and Elazar forced their way through the crowds so the three of them could embrace. The crowd pressed in even closer, everyone eager to see the so-called Messiah for themselves.

I stepped back and watched.

I never got tired of seeing people get excited in the presence of Yeshua.

Excitement was excitement.

Standing in Shimon the Leper's house, watching him and

Elazar, and Myriam and Marta, and everyone else whose lives had been changed by the miracles Yeshua had performed, felt like a taste of heaven.

But I knew it couldn't last.

That was why I felt sick inside.

Dread was in my heart.

59

Tears of Love

I WAS THE first person to notice Myriam come in. She was carrying a heavy stone jar.

Nobody paid her much attention at first, but I saw her.

Yeshua was sitting down at the time, and she approached him purposefully.

This wasn't the first time I'd seen a woman approach Yeshua carrying a bottle of what looked like perfume.

Months ago, when we were in Galilee, a lady had gatecrashed a dinner that a local Pharisee was holding in Yeshua's honour. She'd humbly opened the jar and poured it over his feet, weeping all the time, wiping his feet with her hair.

The whole room fell silent, and the Pharisee took great offence that Yeshua would allow a sinful woman to touch him like that.

Yeshua's response? He told her that her sins were forgiven, at which point, the Pharisee became livid.

But Yeshua simply said what a beautiful thing it was that she had done.

Likewise, Myriam now knelt at Yeshua's feet and got ready to open the bottle. The oil was of great value to her, and Myriam was clearly wanting to do something unique for Yeshua.

Like the woman before, Myriam too had tears in her eyes.

But her tears felt somehow different.

Then she started to pour the oil over the feet of Yeshua and tenderly rubbed it in.

Straight away, Yudah, one of our group, started whining about how Myriam was wasting such an expensive jar of perfume. He said that it would surely be better for the perfume to be sold and the profits given to the poor.

That was Yudah all over. He missed the point.

Unlike me, he hadn't yet surrendered to the will of Yeshua. He always thought he knew a better way. His own way.

That was Yudah's fatal flaw.

I also knew that he was stealing from the money we always set aside for travel. But Yeshua had told me to let it be. So, I did. But I never trusted Yudah again.

Yeshua ignored Yudah's grumblings and turned his attention to Myriam. He had this melancholic expression on his face that made me uncomfortable.

Then I realised what was different about this encounter, from the time before.

It was the smell of the oil.

The first woman's oil had been sweet, like the most beautiful perfume you'd ever encountered. But this time, the smell was almost bitter.

I couldn't put my finger on it.

Yudah was still hovering around, looking annoyed – and he voiced it again.

Then Yeshua said softly, 'Leave her alone. It was intended that she should save this perfume for the day of my burial.'

That was it! It was embalming oil.

Her tears weren't only tears of love – they were tears of grief.

PART FOUR

Yohanan, Friend

Yerushalayim,
C. AD 33

Capital city, site of the holy temple. Governed by a Roman procurator, called Pontius Pilate, tasked with raising taxes for Rome and maintaining law and order.

60

The Donkey (Sunday)

IT WAS THE Sunday before Passover.

It was hot that day.

Passover was still four days away and people were already crowding into the city for the festivities. The Romans were making known their presence in the streets – just like they always did – demonstrating their power and flexing their muscles.

It seemed to me that every corner you turned in the city you saw a soldier glaring back at you.

They always liked to remind their subjects who was really in charge when we gathered for the major festivals.

And this Passover was no different.

Even before we stepped one foot inside the city walls, the Master was making sure that everything was happening the way he wanted it to.

Early in the morning, he sent two of the disciples to a nearby village. He told them they would find a donkey and a colt tied up. The very animal that symbolises service, suffering, peace and humility.

The symbolism wasn't lost on me.

'Bring them to me,' Yeshua had said. 'If anyone asks what you're doing, say, "The Master needs them."'

Soon they were back with both animals, and the Master was finally ready to enter the city one last time.

Just as it was written in the Scriptures some five hundred years earlier:

Tell Zion's daughter: Look, your king's on his way, poised and ready, mounted on a donkey.

It was like Yeshua was fulfilling his destiny, piece by piece.

His story.

61

Praise (Sunday)

I WAS NERVOUS, but the others were excited. Especially when people started to notice the Master on the donkey. Then the gossip started to spread among the gathering crowds.

Who is that?

Is that the prophet Yeshua, the one from Nazaret in Galilee?

The news rippled through the people, lined on either side of the street. Some laid down their cloaks, others were cutting down branches from palm trees and waving them about, before laying them down on the road.

With every few steps the crowd got bigger, and the noise grew louder. I kept an eye out for Roman soldiers, but they seemed to be keeping their distance. There were a few Pharisees trying to blend into the crowds, but even they held back.

As far as I could tell, we were safe for now. There wasn't going to be any lynching yet.

I hated the tension. The fear. It was palpable.

Yet Yeshua seemed somehow calm.

Ready.

Here in the city, death seemed like the last thing on the crowd's mind. The cheers, the smiles and the laughter all appeared completely genuine. People were praising the Master, calling out to Yeshua, greeting him as their long dreamed-of Saviour.

Hosanna to David's son!

Blessed is he who comes in God's name!

Hosanna in highest heaven!

Some of the disciples were loving it – they were probably remembering what it was like when the crowds in Galilee had welcomed and praised Yeshua then too.

Others, like Kephas, Ta'om and especially Yudah, looked wary, like they were troubled by it all.

I could feel my head starting to ache from the pressure. I wanted to do everything right. I wanted to make sure that the Master's wishes were carried out exactly as he wanted, but I also wanted us to get away from here.

I had a hunch that things could turn ugly at any moment.

I glanced across at Yeshua – sitting there, swaying gently on the donkey, his feet almost touching the ground. The faintest trace of a smile on his face.

I never did get to ask him about what was going through his mind that day, but now I have an idea.

How all this would change so fast.

After the Master finished his ride on the donkey up by the temple, he spent the day with everyday people, talking, listening and teaching.

His message was clear.

He was going to be lifted up from the earth. That he was going to be killed – for us all.

But no one seemed to take it on board as reality. No one appeared to understand or believe – it was like the true implication of what was playing out in front of us all fell like sand through people's fingers.

Yeshua had told us that this would happen. But I too had been blind to what the prophet Isaiah had warned:

For this people's heart has become calloused . . . Otherwise, they might see with their eyes, hear with their ears, understand with their hearts and turn, and I would heal them.

62

Pressure (Monday)

THAT SUNDAY EVENING, we went back to Beth 'Anya, and early the next morning, we returned once more to Yerushalayim.

Today, I could tell Yeshua was nervous at what lay ahead. It was written all over him.

Who wouldn't be? He had told us often what would lie ahead.

I remembered Yeshua's haunting words to us: 'For God so loved the world that he gave his one and only Son . . .'

No wonder his heart was troubled.

And I could sense it in him.

On our way, we walked past a bushy fig tree, and Yeshua went over to it to pick fruit from it to eat for breakfast. But he found the tree full only with leaves.

No figs in sight.

Yeshua cursed the tree and turned away from it angrily, walking away, lost in his thoughts. 'No one is going to eat fruit from you again – ever!' He spat out the words under his breath.

Anxious, hungry. And on edge. Yeshua's mood got darker the closer we got to the city.

Once we dropped down the hill that leads into Gad Smane, we stopped in a small garden there, looking out at the city beyond.

Yeshua then dropped to his knees and started to weep openly. I had never seen him like this.

When he caught his breath, his voice was full of pain.

'If you had only recognised this day, and everything that was good for you. But now it's too late.'

He looked as if he was in great turmoil.

None of us knew what to do or say.

He just kept talking out loud. To the city and its future.

'In the days ahead, your enemies are going to surround you . . . They'll smash you and your babies on the pavement. Not one stone will be left intact. All this because you didn't recognise and welcome God's personal visit.'

For the longest time we stood there, staring at the Master while he shouted at the wind. I hated seeing him like this. It was like a great weight was pressing down on him. And that pressure was building.

Eventually, Yeshua got to his feet again and we set off. He was walking quickly now, and the closer he got to the temple, the faster he went. By the time we reached the outer courts, he burst right in like a hurricane.

He stood still for a moment.

His eyes were wild-eyed.

He was breathing heavily. Glaring at the scene in front of him.

The priests selling the animals for sacrifice, taking only the temple currency as payment.

The money changers fleecing people as they exchanged their denarii for the temple coins.

And the people themselves, desperate to do the right thing by God and offer their sacrifices, but struggling to raise enough money to meet the prices.

It was a perfectly contrived black market, designed and authorised by the temple priests themselves. A get-rich-quick scheme that was lining the pockets of the ones who claimed to be God's representatives on earth, right in the very place where we were told that God himself was living.

This money changing system in the outer courts of the temple wasn't new. The Master had seen it before – we all had – but at that moment on that day, it was like someone had opened a tomb and the stench of death and decay was seeping out.

I looked at the Master. His eyes were narrowed, his breathing heavy and his fists clenched.

He was full of rage, and he could only hold it in so long.

Then, he opened his mouth and screamed.

63

Rage and Love (Monday)

YESHUA WENT WILD. He was completely enraged.

He ran into the temple and started yelling. 'It's written in Scripture, "My house is a house of prayer". You have turned it into a den of thieves.'

He was throwing over the merchants' tables, scattering their coins all over the floor. Some of them tried to hold Yeshua back, but they were unable to.

He was like a whirlwind.

I stood to the side and watched in awe.

This fight, this rage, it was real.

And part of me loved seeing him like this.

It felt like it had been brewing in him for weeks now.

Yeshua seemed more like a prophet from the old days than our laid back, belly laughing friend that we knew so well. Here he was, calling down judgement with God's full authority. Raging against corruption. Because his people deserved better.

When every merchant table had been thrown over and every money changer chased out, the Master stood still, panting breathlessly. Eyes still raging. Sweat was dripping from his forehead.

He may have finished with the shouting and the fury, but he wasn't ready to leave the temple. He just stood there, looking back at the hundreds of people who were now staring at him, as if this was the first time he'd noticed them.

Nobody moved a muscle. Everyone was staring at Yeshua in disbelief at what had just happened.

Then the silence was broken by the sound of shuffling footsteps.

They belonged to a group of beggars entering the temple; they had some blind cripples tagging along with them too.

181

Beforehand, most of these invalids had been huddled outside the temple, hoping to receive alms from those leaving.

The Master softened as he looked at this ragged bunch of outcasts approaching him.

When they were close enough, he reached out and touched them. One after another. Immediately, before a single word was spoken, the miracles started happening. Sight was restored. Limbs were made whole.

Life was being handed back to those who had lived so long in suffering. Freely given to those in desperation, who came to him for their healing.

Even though I had witnessed such moments many times before, I had never seen so many miracles happen in such short a time. There were sobs and gasps and screams of joy and gratitude. It was the sound of people whose lives were being transformed in person by the Almighty.

And then I saw the children running.

Masses of them, running up to Yeshua, dancing, singing, praising. They couldn't help themselves.

Calling out to Yeshua, 'Hosanna! Hosanna!'

The words of the Scripture being fulfilled:

Through the praise of children and infants you have established a stronghold against your enemies

My heart felt on fire within me.

64

Dead Wood (Tuesday)

AFTER RETURNING ONCE more to Beth 'Anya, we woke early.

The tension of the previous morning was gone. Yeshua was laughing and talking with us all. Like old times.

I was hoping for a calmer, more ordinary day.

But this day was about to prove far from ordinary.

We set out from Beth 'Anya, following the same route back to the temple. When we reached the fig tree that Yeshua had cursed at the day before, I stopped abruptly, and I stared at it.

Yeshua, on the other hand, didn't even given it a second glance as he swept on past.

But I was shocked.

On Monday, the tree had looked healthy enough. Even though it didn't have any fruit on it, the branches had been strong, and its leaves were thick. Today, it was as dead as a skeleton. The leaves lay curled and withered on the ground. The branches were parched and brittle.

It was finished. In just one day. Good only for firewood.

I don't know why I was surprised, but somehow this small thing shook me up. I think it was because everything I had ever seen Yeshua do was constructive, yet this was the first time I'd seen him use his power for anything destructive.

But it spoke to me of his humanness. It was somehow reassuringly normal that he was like us after all. He got frustrated, he got sad and he got mad.

Like at the fig tree.

Fully divine. Yet fully human.

Seeing that tree also reminded me of the reality of who we were with. That we were truly walking in the presence of a man of supernatural power.

A man who I had seen too often declare himself as the Son of God.

I realised that everything seemed to dance to his tune. The wind, the waves, the trees. The restoring of sight and limbs, the expelling of demons and the feeding of the many.

It made my head spin to think of it.

This man could do it all – and he did. Where there was need, he gave himself.

I gave a quick glance back to the withered stump and hurried to join the others. We pushed on up the last steep hill before dropping down into the Kidron Valley towards Gad Smane.

The olive grove there was busy already when we reached it mid-morning. People were lining up with their sacks full of olives, ready to have them crushed and pressed and turned into oil.

Nobody paid us much notice as we walked by.

We carried on down the valley and ascended to the temple through the Beautiful Gate. We were sweaty and dusty when we arrived, but the Master barely paused.

He just walked straight into the temple and started talking to people who were hanging around the outer court. I noticed that the money changers and merchants that the Master had driven out the day before were nowhere to be seen.

It didn't take long for the Pharisees and priests to come up and start harassing Yeshua.

'Show us your credentials. Who authorised you to teach here?'

But the Master wasn't fazed at all. He just calmly talked to them and then went back to his teaching.

But what he then said made them madder than I'd ever seen them before.

65

Snakes (Tuesday)

'THERE WAS A landowner who planted a vineyard.' Yeshua was speaking directly to the crowd who were sitting around him.

'Then he rented the vineyard to some farmers and moved to another place. When the harvest time approached, he sent his servants to the tenants to collect his fruit. The tenants seized his servants; they beat one, killed another and stoned a third. Then he sent other servants to them, more than the first time, and the tenants treated them in the same way.'

He paused to let the story so far sink in.

'Last of all, he sent his son to them. "They will respect my son," he said. But when the tenants saw the son, they said to each other, "This is the heir. Come, let's kill him and take his inheritance." So, they took him and threw him out of the vineyard and killed him.'

Yeshua paused for effect.

'Therefore, when the owner of the vineyard comes, what will he do to those tenants?'

I kept my eyes on the priests.

The story was so obviously geared at them.

With Yeshua's question hanging in the air, the priests looked like they were about to explode.

'Well, he should bring those wretches to a wretched end,' shouted someone in the crowd.

'Rent the vineyard to other tenants?' said another.

People laughed at that.

The Master smiled.

He looked carefully at the priests and then the crowd. But when he spoke again, we all knew who he was talking to.

'The kingdom of God will be taken away from you and given to a people who will produce its fruit.'

The priests and the Pharisees were holding in their rage. But they could do nothing here.

The people in the crowd were loving this. If the priests tried to make a move on the Master, it would have been anarchy. So they just stood there, seething.

Instead they tried to turn the tables on him, firing off a series of questions designed to trap Yeshua, starting with the thorny issue of whether we should pay taxes to Caesar.

This would divide the crowd, they must have thought.

But Yeshua, knowing their intent, said, 'You hypocrites, why are you trying to trap me? Show me the coin used for paying the tax.'

They brought him a denarius, and he asked them, 'Whose image is this? And whose inscription?'

'Caesar's,' they replied.

Then he said to them simply, 'So give back to Caesar what is Caesar's, and to God what is God's.'

That silenced them for a moment.

But then they tried again. They asked Yeshua, 'What's the most important commandment in all the laws given through Moses?'

Yeshua was quick with that one too:

'"Love the Lord your God with all your heart and with all your soul and with all your mind." This is the first and greatest commandment.' He paused.

'And the second is like it: "Love your neighbour as yourself". All the Law and the Prophets hang on these two commandments.'

At every turn, every answer that the Master gave left them stunned. They were no match for him.

Finally, when Yeshua was done with the ripostes to the Pharisees and priests, he turned to the crowd.

'Watch out for the religious scholars. They love to walk around in academic gowns, preen in the radiance of public flattery, bask in prominent positions, sit at the head table at every function. And all the time they are exploiting the weak and helpless. The longer their prayers, the worse they get.'

He paused.

186

'But they'll pay for it in the end.'

Then he turned back to the Pharisees and priests and gave them his harshest words yet:

'You snakes! You brood of vipers! How will you escape being condemned?' No one dared reply. And Yeshua wasn't finished.

'You make yourselves look good in front of people. But God knows what is really in your hearts.' He paused. 'What people think is important is worth nothing to God.'

Then he got straight up and left.

66

Destroy the Temple (Tuesday)

THOSE OF US disciples raced out after Yeshua.

There would be trouble in the air now. I was certain of that.

We caught up with him outside.

Yeshua stood there, calmly looking back at the temple.

'Do you see all these things?' he said. 'Not one stone here will be left on another; every one will be thrown down.'

That got a lot of the wider group of followers talking.

They asked the Master when all this destruction would happen.

For some of them, all the talk of destroyed buildings was exactly what they wanted to hear. They took it as confirmation that the Master was going to bring some kind of massive revolution that would kick out the Romans and restore the country once and for all.

I kept quiet. I was sure they were wrong.

Yeshua never let anyone second guess him.

Like the time, only a few days before we'd arrived in Yerushalayim, when something happened with Yeshua and me that made me wince.

My mother had gone up to him and asked the kind of thing that only a mother could ask.

She'd tried to get him to promise that when all this was over and we were dead and buried, that both me and my brother Yakov would be given places of honour – sitting on either side of the Master in heaven.

I should have guessed his response.

'You have no idea what you're asking,' Yeshua had said to her gently. Then, turning to Yakov and me, he asked, 'Are you capable of drinking the cup that I'm about to drink?'

We stayed silent after that.

It reminded me of the time that some of the other disciples had been arguing with each other over who would be the greatest in the kingdom of God one day.

It had been foolish talk round a meal.

Yet Yeshua had silenced that one too.

He called a little child to him, and carefully placed the child among us. Then he said, 'The truth is, you must change your thinking and become like little children. If you don't do this, you will never enter God's kingdom.'

That had us all confused for a second.

Then he added, 'The greatest person in God's kingdom is the one who makes himself humble like this child.'

That was the way of Yeshua. Topside down. Bottom side up. Turning the tables and re-writing conventional thinking.

Yeshua had told us that to be the greatest, we had to make ourselves the least.

'Be a servant to all. Love your neighbour as yourself,' he had said.

It was revolutionary talk. But a different kind of revolution to which many aspired.

His was a revolution of love.

That's not to say there wasn't also talk of judgement.

In fact, ever since Yeshua had ridden into Yerushalayim, he had spent a lot of his time talking about judgement.

Listing the ways that so many of the Pharisees and the priests were failing both God and the people. In truth, he was speaking about us all.

Even the fig tree that I'd seen that morning reminded me of God's frustration at those of us who looked good but bore no fruit.

The Master had brought his judgement down on that tree, and now it was withered and dead.

But there was something else I'd noticed about Yeshua. In all his stories, there was a solution. Like the landowner, who hadn't just walked away from the problem but had sent his own son to deal with it. It was the son who had fixed the problem, even though it resulted in his death.

The Master might be talking about judgement, but he was also talking about the resolution.

That *he* would pay the ultimate price.

It wasn't just revolution that he was bringing. It was sacrifice.

If there had been any doubt in my mind about Yeshua's intentions, that doubt vanished within hours of returning to Beth 'Anya.

It was early evening, and Yeshua called us together and sat us down. He was as solemn as I'd ever seen him.

'You know that Passover comes in two days,' he said.

His voice rich with emotion. Yet strangely calm.

'The Son of Man will soon be delivered over to the chief priests and the teachers of the law.'

He held his words. Then he continued.

'They will condemn him to death and will hand him over to the Gentiles . . . to be mocked and flogged and crucified.'

No one dared speak. Not a whisper.

Yeshua had warned us of this, but only in looser terms.

This time there was no doubt. No hidden meanings.

It was as plain as could be.

They will hand the Son of Man over to be mocked and flogged and crucified.

He let the silence hang a moment, then smiled and added:

'But on the third day he will be raised to life!'

67

Betrayal (Wednesday)

EVERYONE ALWAYS HAD their own opinions of the Master.

Some thought that when he drove the money changers out of the temple, the Master was finally heading in the right direction.

Some thought that he shouldn't have been going after fellow Israelites at all, but that he should have concentrated instead on the Romans, who were the real enemy.

And there were some of us who thought that all of this was just another example of the Master doing what the Master always did. Helping us to find the truth and to see the beauty in it all.

I can't tell you for sure which of these camps Yudah belonged to. Maybe he was in a bit of all three.

All of us get confused and feel lost at times.

But I couldn't help feeling that Yudah ultimately thought he knew best.

What I do know for certain is that today, when the Master and the rest of us were sitting on the Mount of Olives just near Gad Smane, Yudah wasn't there.

He was walking back towards the city.

Keeping in the shadows, ducking down alleyways and staying out of sight.

He knew exactly where he was going.

Towards the temple. To talk to the priests.

He had a plan.

The priests weren't in the outer courts, so he had to go to some of the temple soldiers who were on guard.

'I need to see the high priest,' Yudah said quietly.

The guards were suspicious. They'd seen him there the previous two days with the Master and suspected he was trouble.

He was.

But not for them.

Yudah insisted it would be in their interest. Trust him, he told them. And eventually they relented.

The guards cautiously escorted Yudah in for a meeting with representatives of the high priest himself.

They recognised him instantly and called the priests to join them.

And unlike the guards on the gate, the priests understood that if Yudah wanted to meet them like this, then he wasn't fully loyal to Yeshua.

Whether Yudah could be trusted or not, time would tell – but he could be used. And the priests and their representatives knew it.

They offered him a seat. Brought out wine and figs.

'I can help you,' said Yudah nervously.

'Who says we need it?'

'Anyone who's been in the temple these last two days has heard what Yeshua has been saying. Calling you vipers and hypocrites. By now, everyone in the city thinks that you can't control him.'

Yudah let the words sink in, then continued.

'How long before the crowd turns against you? How long then, before the Romans deem that you're no use to them?'

That was the clincher.

The gathering said nothing.

Yudah leaned forward and lowered his voice. 'I can help. Don't you see it?'

He paused.

'I can hand him over to you.'

'And what would we do with him?' they replied nonchalantly.

Yudah knew the game they were playing. He could play it too.

'That's then up to you,' Yudah responded. He was looking around warily.

The priests talked quietly among themselves.

They knew this was their chance.

'And how much would you want for your service?' they asked, almost as if the answer was academic.

Yudah had a number. In fact, he'd been thinking about it all week. Fifteen pieces of silver was a lot of money, at least two months' wages. It was more than fair.

But now that he was here, sitting in the opulent room, facing these bloated high priests with their ceremonial robes and expensive jewels, drinking fine wine from Roman cups, he changed his mind.

He went bigger.

Whether or not Yudah ever wanted any genuine harm to come to Yeshua, I will never know.

Maybe Yudah was simply frightened – for himself, for where all Yeshua's actions were leading. Maybe he believed that the message, the mission, was more important than just one man.

Maybe he felt Yeshua's sense of self, of his own importance, was blinding everyone to the reality of this precarious situation.

Maybe Yudah simply feared for his own future.

People tell themselves what they want to hear.

But there in that courtyard, he sold his friend.

For thirty pieces of silver.

68

'Then Not Only My Feet'
(Thursday)

WE AWOKE IN Beth 'Anya once more, and I knew today would be special.

It was Passover night, and the Master had everything planned out.

Instead of remaining outside the city with Myriam, Marta and Elazar, the Master told us we were going somewhere new.

He gave Kephas a thorough set of instructions that included meeting a man carrying a water jug and following him home. Kephas did as he was told, and soon he was showing us into a spacious, second-story room in the heart of the city.

It would be here that we would feast together.

I had no idea of what really lay ahead.

For us closest disciples, I'd hoped this day would be a simple time of Passover celebration. A time to put the dramas of the last few days behind us and to recover. To eat, to feast, and to celebrate with Yeshua and our friends.

Just as we had done at this festival for the last few years.

By the time the sun set that evening and all twelve of us were gathered in the room with him, our Passover anticipation was high.

The table was set just as it should be. There were the bitter herbs, the lamb, the wine, the unleavened bread. It was all so beautifully done and so familiar.

But just when we were starting to get settled, the Master spoke.

'You've no idea how much I have looked forward to eating this Passover meal with you . . .'

He smiled at each of us in turn. So . . . unrushed.

As if this moment had long been anticipated.

Foretold.

Then Yeshua took a slow breath.

'Before I enter my time of suffering . . . It's the last one I'll eat until we all eat it together in the kingdom of God.'

We all looked at each other. Confused.

I knew Yeshua had been speaking of this for some time. But part of me had kept wondering if he had been maybe speaking in some sort of code. That he meant something else.

The words of being handed over and killed being some metaphor for life. Like that time when he spoke to Nicodemus about being reborn.

That conversation felt so long ago now.

A heavy silence settled around our Passover table.

Then Yeshua slowly took a cup of wine and gave thanks to God. Then he stood up from the table, removed his robe and did something I could never have anticipated.

He picked up a small towel and a bowl of warm water that had been set aside, then he knelt and started washing my feet.

I didn't know how to react. What to say.

I looked at the others nervously.

Then he moved on to Yakov. Then to Mattias. Andreas.

Still, no one said a word.

When Yeshua reached Kephas, the burly fisherman spoke up. As only Kephas can.

'Master, are you really going to wash my feet?'

Yeshua didn't even look up. He simply held Kephas' feet in his hands and replied, 'You don't understand now what I'm doing, but it will be clear enough to you later.'

Kephas pulled his feet away abruptly.

'No, Master! You're not going to wash my feet – ever!'

Yeshua looked up at him, square in the eye, and replied, 'If I don't wash you, you can't be part of what I'm doing.'

Kephas looked taken aback for a moment. But after he'd thought things through, he threw his arms wide and exclaimed, 'Not only my feet, then. Wash my hands! Wash my head!'

Yeshua laughed. Our good friend Kephas.

This washing wasn't about hygiene. It was about being made clean inside – not just outside.

Made holy, forgiven before God.

Yeshua spoke as he washed Kephas' feet. 'If you've had a bath in the morning, you only need your feet washed now and you're clean from head to toe. So now you're clean.'

Kephas nodded and looked down at his clean feet. So moved. Yeshua then continued round the group, and finally sat back down next to me.

For a moment it felt like time was slowing down.

I placed my hand on the small of Yeshua's back. I wanted this to last forever. All of us together. Him among us. An intimacy, connection and friendship I had dreamt of all my life.

'Do you understand what I have done to you?' Yeshua then said.

'You address me as "Teacher" and "Master", and rightly so. That is what I am.'

He paused.

'So, if I, the Master and Teacher, washed your feet, you must now wash each other's feet. I've laid down a pattern for you. What I've done, you do.'

Everyone nodded, a little uncertain about what he meant.

Yeshua tried to explain: 'I'm only pointing out the obvious. A servant is not ranked above his master; an employee doesn't give orders to the employer.'

He smiled at us all and concluded, 'If you understand what I'm telling you, act like it, and live a blessed life.'

It wasn't the usual way to kick off a Passover feast. That was sure. No talk of Moses leading the Israelites out of Egypt, or of slaves being released.

But that was nothing compared to what happened next.

It was time now for the Master to share out the Passover bread and the wine.

The matzo and the four small cups – the symbols of deliverance and freedom.

Yeshua held the unleavened bread, blessed it, broke it into pieces and started handing them out.

But what he said was a shock.

'This is my body,' he said, looking each of us in the eye. 'Given for you.' He paused. 'Eat it in my memory.'

Eat his body? That was not part of any Passover feast.

None of us could even imagine something so wretched and unclean.

It got stranger when he picked up the cup.

'This cup is the new covenant written in my blood; blood poured out for you.'

Drink his blood?

Every year we had celebrated Passover together. And I can assure you, Yeshua had never said anything as radical as this before.

Nobody knew how to respond. We all just sat there. Confused.

But the Master had a look in his eyes that told us he wasn't joking, so we nibbled the bread tentatively and sipped the wine.

Kephas typically just downed his.

Then we waited for the next bombshell. It came quickly.

'I have something hard but important to say to you,' Yeshua then said.

He held his gaze on each of us.

'Believe me when I say that one of you twelve here will hand me over to my enemies.'

69

'Don't Play Games with Me'
(Thursday)

THE MOOD CHANGED immediately.

A ripple of disbelief, then everyone started talking at once. Everybody telling the Master that surely this could not be the truth. That they would never be the one to betray him.

But Yeshua was barely listening. He kept his eyes locked on the table.

He only looked up when he heard these words:

'It isn't me, is it, Rabbi?'

Yeshua locked his eyes on the speaker. Yudah – Yudah of Kerioth.

The Master stared at him hard.

'Don't play games with me, Yudah.'

We were all confused.

If you'd asked me a few months back, Yudah just hadn't seemed the type to betray him. He oversaw the money. We trusted him.

Well, all of us except Kephas, who had never got on well with Yudah, but Kephas himself could be difficult and opinionated at times. We all knew that.

The Master then slumped forward, like a great weight was suddenly on his back. I put my arm around him. This was not how I had imagined the celebration to be going.

I asked him gently, 'Master, who?'

Yeshua looked up, took a deep breath and spoke. His voice was laced with emotion.

'The one to whom I give this crust of bread . . .'

Everybody stared as he picked up a hunk of bread from the

table and reached out for the wine. He held the crust in the wine for a second then pulled it out.

He held it there for a while, the red wine dripping from the bread down onto his hands.

We all sat there, watching. Waiting.

Then Yeshua leaned over and handed the wine-stained bread to Yudah.

For a moment nothing happened.

The Master still holding out the bread and Yudah frozen in place.

Drops of blood-red wine still dripping onto the table.

Since that night I've sometimes wondered what would have happened if Yudah had stayed like that. What if he'd refused to take the bread?

But it seemed that everything was already in motion. The betrayal was underway. Yudah's deal already done.

'What you must do, do,' said the Master to Yudah in a much firmer, sterner voice. 'Do it and get it over with.'

Yudah reached out, snatched the bread, then left.

70

'The Love You Have for Each Other' (Thursday)

AS SOON AS Yudah left the room, everyone took a breath and looked around at each other. Then the Master appeared to relax. As if a weight had been lifted from us all.

But Yeshua's words were still solemn and full of warning.

'I am with you for only a short time longer.' He looked at us each in turn. 'Then I am going to the one who sent me.'

Those were painful words to hear for me. I had spent three years following him. I had left my family and my livelihood behind so that I could be with him as he travelled around the country.

I'd gone with him from town to town, village to village, standing by his side as he healed the sick and taught people about how to live right by God. I'd given up everything to be by his side.

And now?

When we needed him the most, in all this turmoil and confusion, he was just going to leave?

I felt sick inside.

Why would you leave now? We can still do this – we can do it all together. You can use your power, surely? I've seen it so often. Don't give up. Not in the face of these weak, religious zealots.

I had spent so long following Yeshua that I simply couldn't imagine what life would be like without him. Without his presence. His laughter, his sense of mischief and his tough spirit that never complained, even when we were done in, beat with exhaustion.

The thought of looking for the Master but not being able to find him was hell to me.

But before I could verbalise any of this, he kept talking to us.

It felt as if he had so much that he still wanted us to know. So much still to share.

'Let me give you a new command: love one another. In the same way I loved you, you love one another. This is how everyone will recognise that you are my disciples – when they see the love you have for each other.'

The words seemed to float in the air around us.

And in time that one message would become so important to us.

We would all return to it again and again in the years to come.

Those words would give us strength and hope and resolve.

But right then, in the darkened room, with the Passover feast still unfinished on the table before us, they were so hard to absorb properly.

I just wanted to know what was going to happen.

It was Ta'om who had the courage to speak up first.

'Master, we have no idea where you're going. How do you expect us to know the road?'

Yeshua gently got up and went and sat next to Ta'om, then he looked at us all. He seemed so unrushed.

'I am the way, the truth and the Life. No one comes to the Father except through me.'

He paused.

'If you really knew me, you would know my Father as well. From now on, you do know him. You've even seen him!'

Before we could even comprehend all this, Kephas jumped in and asked the same question as Ta'om.

'Master, exactly *where* are you going?'

Yeshua smiled. He always loved Kephas and his no-nonsense spirit. Always straight to the point.

'You can't now follow me where I'm going.' He held his words then added, 'You will follow later.'

But Kephas didn't let it go.

'Master,' he said, his arms now wide and voice pleading, just like he had been that night out on the lake when we'd all seen Yeshua walk on the water, 'I'm ready for anything with you. I'd go to jail for you. I'd die for you!'

'O Shimon, Shimon. I have prayed that you will not lose your faith!'

Kephas instantly replied: 'All the others may lose their faith, but my faith will never be shaken.'

There was a pause. A long one.

Then words from the Master which made Kephas recoil in fear.

'Before the rooster crows, you will have three times denied that you know me.'

71

'The World Will No Longer See Me' (Thursday)

IT FELT AS if we were hurtling towards a cliff and we were totally out of control.

There seemed to be no way that any of us could stop all these disastrous predictions. I felt a sense of panic rising within me.

This can't be unravelling like this.

If this was the Master's last meal, I hated it. This wasn't what I'd hoped would happen. I stared at the table. I was scared.

I tried to remember where we were in the Passover feast. To re-plant myself in something familiar.

The Master had long stopped following the traditional Passover pattern. And all hope of a celebration together had been shattered.

But then it hit me.

I began to see what the Master was doing. Why he had chosen that night of all nights to do it.

It wasn't a coincidence that he would eat his final meal at Passover.

If ever there was a moment when people were reflecting on being rescued and set on the path to freedom, Passover was it.

But our people never found true freedom. We left Egypt, but we remained slaves. Slaves to our repeated mistakes. Our shortcomings. Under the heel of our enemies.

We celebrated Passover every year, but our journey was incomplete.

Now it appeared that the Master was about to change that.

After Yeshua had told Kephas that he'd deny him three times that very night, Kephas had sat distraught.

Kephas was the Master's most loyal friend and his fiercest defender.

He might be prone to saying a few impulsive things from time to time, but denying that he even knew the Master? And three times? That surprised me. I could never imagine that happening.

But the Master didn't lie, and he never made mistakes.

Kephas looked like he'd just had his heart ripped out of his chest, and he hardly touched his food after that. But the rest of us started to eat, and the wine and food went some of the way to calm the atmosphere that had been so charged beforehand.

Then the Master started talking again. He spoke of love, and that we should not let any of this rattle us.

He said there was plenty of room for all of us in his Father's home and that he was going to 'get our room ready' and then come back to collect us.

To some, it might have sounded like another story. To me, he was simply making a promise.

Then Yeshua closed his eyes and spoke out loud: 'Father I pray that all who believe in me will be one. You are in me and I am in you.'

He breathed deeply. Then he looked around at us.

'All who love me will obey my teaching. My Father and I will come to them and live with them.' He paused. 'I have told you these things while I am with you. But the Helper will teach you everything and cause you to remember all that I told you. This Helper is the Holy Spirit that the Father will send in my name.'

He let the words sink in. Then he reached out to put his hands on our shoulders.

'I leave you peace. It is my own peace I give you. I give you peace in a different way than the world does. So don't be troubled.' He smiled. 'Don't be afraid.'

The Master was looking intently at all of us as he spoke, even Kephas.

'I will not leave you orphaned,' he said. 'I'm coming back.' He held our hands in his at this point.

'In just a little while, the world will no longer see me, but you're going to see me because I am alive and you're about to come alive.'

We all looked at each other but said nothing.

'In this world you will have troubles. But be brave! I have defeated the world!' He was smiling now.

Then the Master pushed himself up from where he sat and briskly said, 'Get up. Let's go. It's time to leave.'

72

'May this Cup Be Taken from Me' (Thursday)

IT WAS DARK outside, but there was just enough moonlight to walk by. The streets were empty, and the air had a chill to it.

I felt a sense of trepidation in the pit of my stomach that I couldn't shift.

Everything felt cold that night. And even the city was strangely quiet.

The Master led us quickly and quietly down into the Kidron Valley. It was the same route that we'd walked twice a day since Sunday.

The temple walls were like shadows above us. Shadows that we could never hope to climb. We walked in silence, and I couldn't stop thinking about the words he'd said on Tuesday, not far from where we were now passing.

'Not one stone here will be left on another; every one will be thrown down.'

We carried on towards the Mount of Olives. I wondered whether we were going to walk all the way back to Beth 'Anya again. Part of me hoped that we were. It would be safer there.

But the Master stopped when we were only just out of the city, in the garden near Gad Smane.

He told the others to stay where they were, then took Kephas, Yakov and myself with him, further into the olive grove.

We walked with him. Side by side. Slowly. Through the garden. No rush. Breathing in and breathing out. As if Yeshua was savouring every moment of this beautiful still night.

As he ambled among the olive trees, I saw him looking up at the moon. He seemed to be admiring it somehow.

I noticed the clouds were rolling in now across the sky. Unstoppable.

My head was full of thoughts and my heart full of emotion. I was terrified of what lay ahead.

Then Yeshua stopped and slumped slowly, knee by knee, to the ground. As if he was in pain suddenly. He was bent right over on all fours.

And then I heard muffled weeping. The weight of what he was feeling overwhelming him, like a thousand rocks falling upon him.

'Master, are you all right?' I asked him. 'What can we do?'

'My heart is so heavy with grief; I feel as if I am dying,' he whispered.

He fell silent.

Then he lifted his head and looked right at me.

'Wait here and stay awake with me.'

So, we did. The three of us sat as he moved beneath a nearby tree.

He prayed, mumbled words through a broken voice. We went to him and placed our hands on his back as he lay on the ground shaking.

Then he suddenly stirred into life and prayed out loud.

'My Father, if it is possible, may this cup be taken from me.' His voice was like a wounded animal, raw with pain.

His chest was heaving now.

Slowly it settled and I heard him whisper.

'Yet not as I will, but as you will.'

After that there was silence.

The three of us sat down and watched, hunched tight in our cloaks from the cold night chill. We watched the Master praying. He barely moved. He just lay where he was, face down in the dirt.

Each of us slipped deeper into our thoughts and fears. And I found myself dozing off. I could not help it.

Just then, the Master's voice jolted me awake. He was standing over us. I had to rub the sleep out of my eyes to see clearly.

He was talking directly to Kephas.

'Could you men not stay awake with me for one hour?'

Yeshua looked sick with worry now. 'Stay awake and pray for strength against temptation. Your spirit wants to do what is right, but your body is weak.'

His words went deep into the three of us. I felt such shame.

He then turned and went back to where he'd been lying down and praying. And just like before, he started to groan quietly, calling out in despair to God.

We stayed awake as best we could. We heard him pray. Over and over. The same words.

'May your will be done.'

'May your will be done.'

I swore I saw his forehead glistening with blood, as if he was somehow sweating raw fear.

I tried to pray once more. Twice as hard as before.

I knelt beside him and asked God for another way. To spare the Master. I prayed for help. For God's leagues of angels to rescue Yeshua. I prayed that none of us would be abandoned.

I prayed it all. Over and over.

But soon I felt my head nod and my eyes close. Then sleep overwhelmed me once more.

Yeshua shook me awake with a jolt. I sat bolt upright.

How long had it been?

How was I unable to do the one, simple thing that he asked of me in his hour of desperation? To stay awake with my Master.

I had failed him again.

Yet Yeshua simply smiled at me. There were no tears in his eyes any longer, and his breathing was now slow and calm.

He knelt beside the others and shook them also by the shoulder.

'Are you going to sleep on and make a night of it?' His voice was gentle but teasing.

'My time is up; I am about to be handed over to the hands of sinners. Get up! Let's get going!'

He took one slow, deep breath, then said quietly:

'My betrayer is here.'

73

The Kiss (Thursday)

ALMOST AT ONCE, we heard footsteps approaching and saw lights ahead.

The lamps cast strange shadows, and it sounded like there were more than a handful of people coming, and by the sound of clinking metal, it meant they were armed.

Then I saw them. There were at least twenty. A mob made up of temple soldiers and local heavies. Everybody, apart from one, had either a sword or heavy stick.

They looked ready to fight. I got ready to run.

Then I recognised one of them. The one man who wasn't armed. It was Yudah.

I was speechless.

He's actually done it.

Yudah couldn't look any of us in the eye. He stood there, frozen. Awkward.

The rest of the disciples with us had the same reaction. Shocked silence and paralysing fear.

And confusion.

Why? What did he want?

It was the Master who broke the silence.

'Who are you after?'

All eyes fell on Yudah. But Yudah stayed in the shadows. Mute.

Eventually it was one of the soldiers who called out, 'Yeshua the Nazarene.'

'That's me,' said the Master softly.

The mob twitched. Some of them recoiled as they heard him speak those words. As if they were suddenly aware of being in the presence of danger.

Yudah then started slowly to move forward, towards Yeshua.

He went right up to him, his eyes locked on him nervously,

then he placed his hands on Yeshua's shoulders and planted a kiss on his cheek.

Yeshua spoke to him. 'Friend, why this charade?'

Then Yudah stepped back and the mob sprang into action. Rushing forward, grabbing and surrounding the Master, like a pack of wild dogs.

It was chaos.

Some of the disciples recoiled back, but others closed in, trying to pull the mob off the Master.

I then saw Kephas throw back his cloak and pull out a blade – the kind of sharp tool as long as your forearm that we'd use on the boats.

In a heartbeat, he was slashing at one of the temple guards. The man screamed and clutched the side of his head.

Then Yeshua let out a loud rebuke: 'Put back your sword.'

Everyone froze.

Then the guard looked at the ground. His ear was glistening in the torchlight.

Yeshua instantly reached down, picked it up and touched the side of the guard's head. And just like that his ear was restored.

The guard looked in shock and glanced at the others around him in confusion.

Yeshua continued in a loud voice to us all, 'Do you think for a minute I'm not going to drink this cup the Father gave me?'

Nobody was moving, nobody knew what to do. Even the guards looked taken aback.

Only the Master stood tall. Then he spoke firmly to us all.

'Put your sword back in its place. People who use swords will be killed with swords. Surely you know I could ask my Father and he would give me more than twelve armies of angels.'

He glared at each of us there. The silence lingered.

Then he continued gently, 'But it must happen this way, to show the truth of what the Scriptures said.'

He took a step forward, put his hands out in front of him and gave himself to the head guard.

Then looking at Yudah: 'Do what you came for.'

As soon as the guard had Yeshua's hands, the rest of the mob instantly switched back to violence.

Fists and the sticks started flying.

They beat the Master across the head until he fell to the ground, and I saw blows then raining down on him. He was curled up in a ball on the ground, covering his head.

The violence of the mob had turned in a second and it was overwhelming. Brutal.

As for us? Almost as one, those of us who called ourselves his disciples, broke free, turned and ran away from the scene.

In his hour of greatest need, we took flight – like a flock of startled birds.

I didn't know what else to do.

When we got out of the olive garden, we paused to catch our breath. We stood there in shock. Silent.

We stayed hidden but nervously tried to look to see what was happening.

All I could decipher was the faint glow of the mob's torches through the trees and the sound of shuffling feet and weapons. Then once more, the repeated sound of sticks hitting Yeshua, as the Master moaned in muffled pain.

Now was my chance to go back and rescue him. It was now or never.

But I was afraid. So afraid. And I was a coward.

So I did what every coward does.

I turned away from the one I loved – from the 'Son of Man' as Yeshua called himself – and ran.

I ran as fast as I could into the night.

74

Blasphemy (Friday)

THE MOB FOLLOWED their instructions and took Yeshua straight to the house of Kaiaphas, the Chief Priest.

It was late, but the place was already full of priests and other leaders.

Waiting.

Even the courtyard outside was crowded, with people gathering around charcoal fires, excitedly drawn by the whispers that had been circulating all evening.

Something was afoot. Something big.

Inside Kaiaphas' house, all eyes were now on Yeshua.

He was hunched over from the beating, and his hands were bound tight behind his back with thick, rough rope.

There was blood dripping off his head, and heavy swelling was visible across his face.

Slowly, he lifted his head and tried to breathe. He looked at his accusers and waited.

Stood there in front of him were Kaiaphas and the members of the Jewish Council.

They were talking quietly among themselves. Envy is a sorrowful master to serve. And Yeshua's growing influence and popularity, his claims of being the Messiah, his reckless activities on Shabbat, his supposed healings . . . it was all creating too much unwanted attention – and in the wrong place.

It had to be stopped.

What they wanted was simple enough – the death of Yeshua – but achieving it was more complicated.

Kaiaphas could just have him killed and disposed of – in secret. But Yeshua was widely known, loved by many. Revered. Murdering him would cause chaos at this sensitive time of

Passover. And angry crowds mixed with on-edge Roman soldiers makes for violence and restrictions.

Kaiaphas knew he needed this to be handled in a more subtle, orderly, non-dramatic fashion. Make the problem go away and it will be forgotten.

What Kaiaphas did not want was a revolt on his hands – or to make this Galilean some sort of martyr for freedom.

No. This required careful handling.

The safest way was to get the Romans to have him executed. Then it was done. Off the high priest's plate and conscience, and religious life could resume as normal.

But for that to happen the elite needed evidence that he had broken one of their major laws. And so far, Yeshua had failed to do that.

One by one, the priests gathered in the courtyard, trying to goad Yeshua into saying something they could use against him.

Yeshua simply stayed silent.

Kaiaphas tried a different line of attack.

He nodded to the two soldiers standing either side of him. One then moved behind and roughly tied a piece of cloth around Yeshua's head. The other stood in front, waited until the blindfold was in place and then delivered a hefty blow to Yeshua's head.

Yeshua stumbled, then regained his footing.

He still said nothing.

One of the priests then edged forward and whispered into Yeshua's ear, 'So, you are the Messiah?'

Yeshua turned his head in the direction of the voice.

And this time he replied.

'If I said yes, you wouldn't believe me. If I asked what you meant by your question, you wouldn't answer me.'

Another nod from Kaiaphas.

Another heavy blow landed on Yeshua's other side of his head. This time Yeshua went all the way down.

He struggled slowly back to his feet. Then two men approached Kaiaphas and whispered to him. When Kaiaphas was satisfied, he ushered one of the men to take the floor and speak to Yeshua.

The man took his time, then pointed, arm firmly out-stretched, and exclaimed in a loud voice to all at the gathering:

'He said, "I can tear down this temple of God and after three days rebuild it."'

Kaiaphas himself then took a step towards Yeshua, tore the blindfold off his covered head and looked Yeshua square in the eyes.

'What do you have to say to the accusation?'

Yeshua was silent again.

Kaiaphas couldn't contain his frustration.

'I command you by the authority of the living God to say if you are the Messiah, the Son of God!'

Yeshua slowly lifted his head and replied. 'You said it.'

Then Yeshua turned to face all the others gathered and said with a clear voice, 'And that's not all. Soon you'll see it for yourself. "The Son of Man seated at the right hand of the Mighty One, arriving on the clouds of heaven."'

You didn't have to be a scholar or priest to understand this.

The words were immediately recognisable to everyone present. The clouds of heaven were a sign of divine authority, and the phrase, 'The Son of Man' was from the ancient Scriptures.

It was the name that the prophet Daniel had ascribed hundreds of years earlier to the one that God would use on the final day of judgement.

It took less than a second for Kaiaphas to register what he had heard.

He ripped at his robes, turned round and exclaimed to those gathered, 'He blasphemed! Why do we need witnesses to accuse him? You all heard him blaspheme!'

The room erupted with the words that the priests all longed to hear.

'Death!'

The religious mob now surged around Yeshua. Some spat in his face and others knocked him to the ground.

Once he was on the floor, still bound, they kicked him over and over.

75

'What Must I do?'

THE WORDS THAT Yeshua had once been asked kept repeating inside my head. I couldn't shake them.

'What must I do to inherit eternal life?'

I could hear the question like it had been asked to him only yesterday. But this encounter between Yeshua and the legal expert had happened many months earlier.

It was late afternoon, and the legal scholar had been quizzing Yeshua for some time. The man appeared to be enjoying the intellectual tussle between himself and the Master.

Yeshua never shied away from such mental jousting. Let them ask their questions, was how he always saw it. *They must ask.*

I can't even remember where we were at the time, but I certainly remember the final question that this lawyer put to the Master:

'What must I do to inherit eternal life?'

We all looked at Yeshua. Intrigued at what he would say in reply.

'What is written in the law?' he had said. 'How do you read it?'

The lawyer answered, '"Love the Lord your God with all your heart and with all your soul and with all your strength and with all your mind"; and "Love your neighbour as yourself."'

The man looked pleased with his reply. And we were impressed as well.

'You have answered correctly,' Yeshua replied. 'Do this and you will live.' At that, Yeshua started to stand, and we readied ourselves to move off.

But the man stopped Yeshua. He wanted more. So he asked the Master, 'And who is my neighbour?'

We all looked back at Yeshua. In anticipation. This would be interesting.

Yeshua smiled, took a deep breath and told this story.

'A man was going down from Yerushalayim to Yericho when he was attacked by robbers. They stripped him of his clothes, beat him and went away, leaving him half dead.'

Yeshua looked around, letting the words settle.

'A priest happened to be going down the same road, and when he saw the man, he passed by on the other side. So too, a Levite, when he came to the place and saw him, passed by on the other side. But a Samaritan, as he travelled, came where the man was; and when he saw him, he took pity on him. He went to him and bandaged his wounds, pouring on oil and wine. Then he put the man on his own donkey, brought him to an inn and took care of him.'

The lawyer was looking less assured at this point. But Yeshua continued.

'The next day, the Samaritan took out two silver denarii and gave them to the innkeeper. 'Look after him,' he said, 'and when I return, I will reimburse you for any extra expense you may have.'

Yeshua paused for effect.

Then he asked us all, 'Which of these three do you think was a neighbour to the man who fell into the hands of robbers?'

The lawyer replied reluctantly, 'The one who had mercy on him.'

Yeshua looked him in the eye, smiled and told him, 'Go and do likewise.'

Those words. *Go and do likewise.*

All I could think of now was Yeshua, bound and being beaten by the authorities.

I had so wanted to be his neighbour.

But I had failed him.

76

The Betrayal (Friday)

AFTER YESHUA'S INITIAL arrest in Gad Smane, I had followed the tail end of the mob as they had marched him to Kaiaphas' house. Kephas had been with me too, following, both of us keeping to the shadows.

We didn't say anything to each other, but I noticed that he kept one hand tight on his blade.

Both of us had been seen with the Master a lot throughout the week, so when we reached Kaiaphas' house, we were wary of being spotted. But many were gathered, and we easily slipped into the courtyard unnoticed. Hidden among the crowd.

Most of the high priest's staff were just hanging around, relaxing after all the work of the Passover feast.

Kephas and I discreetly split up. I heard that Yeshua was inside, being interrogated.

It was late and cold, but even though there was a fire burning in the middle of the courtyard, I kept away and stayed in the shadows. Not Kephas though. He always hated the cold, so he pulled his hood over his head and went right up to the fire to keep warm.

It was tempting to go over and join Kephas, and the heat from the burning charcoal and the smell of the incense was alluring, but I resisted. We were in dangerous territory here.

Instead, I tried hard to listen to what was going on inside the inner courtyard with Yeshua. From time to time, I could hear shouting and jeers from inside.

But mostly I just sat and waited, and prayed for Yeshua. I didn't know what else to do.

Then suddenly I heard the words that I most dreaded.

'Hey,' said a voice near the fire. 'This man was with him!'

I looked over and saw one of the servant girls pointing directly at Kephas.

Kephas pulled his hood down further over his head.

'Woman, I don't know what you're talking about,' Kephas responded angrily, before shifting away from the fire.

Suddenly another man spoke up as well.

'She's right. You're one of them.'

Again, Kephas denied it. 'I am not,' he said, his voice starting to crack and show signs of fear. 'I swear I am not.'

And at that, Kephas backed right away, to the far edge of the courtyard, and steadfastly remained in the shadows.

I carefully moved across to join him, and together we leant against the cold wall in silence and waited. We were both on edge now, but we had to stay and just hope that Yeshua would soon be released.

For a while there was nothing more to hear. I watched the sky start to get light in the east, and the black of night began to give way to the grey that comes before dawn.

Then something dramatic must have happened, because the whole place suddenly erupted with shouts of abuse and stamping.

It was the distinct sound of violence.

All of us out in the courtyard listened intently. Waiting in anticipation. Kephas asked someone if they knew anything.

It was then that I noticed that one official had his eyes locked on Kephas.

I tugged at Kephas' cloak and told him to move away. But it was too late.

'He's got to have been with him!' the official yelled, standing up and pointing at Kephas.

'He's a Galilean if I've ever heard one. Listen to the man!'

Kephas' provincial northern accent had given him away, and he looked terrified.

'I don't know what you're talking about,' Kephas shouted, as he backed away quickly towards the entrance.

As soon as Kephas had spoken that third denial, there was a piercing sound as a rooster crowed.

Just as the Master had foretold.

Kephas turned and stared at me in horror, as he realised what he had just done.

Then he span on his heels and ran.

77

Death (Friday)

KEPHAS WAS DOUBLED over, crouched low on the ground, and he let out a muffled cry of pain. I knew what Kephas was feeling, because I had felt it myself.

It's the pain of failing those we love.

I had fallen asleep when I had been told to stay awake. I had run when he was taken. I had kept hidden when my Master was being mocked and beaten.

And when my friend here had been discovered, I hid in the shadows.

I was just as much a coward as Kephas. Maybe more so.

The spotting of Kephas had caused some excitement for a while, but it swiftly died down. He was soon forgotten. I put my hand on Kephas' shoulder and told him I was going to go back in and wait.

I had hardly been back inside the courtyard for ten minutes when the inner doors opened and a great crowd of priests bustled out, all bunched together like badly trained soldiers.

The crowd around me surged closer.

'He's a blasphemer!' yelled one of the priests. 'We're taking him to Pilate!'

That was bad news. Pilate was as senior as it was possible to go in this land. The Roman hand of rule over all of us.

I pushed forward, trying to keep my hood up. There, right in the middle of the thick knot of priests, was the Master. I only got the briefest of glimpses, but I could see he was blindfolded and bruised. His hands were tied, and he was being violently pushed and pulled as he was swept along by his captors.

He was silent. He reminded me of an animal being taken off for slaughter.

They hurried out of the courtyard and headed off towards Pilate's official residence.

I followed cautiously at a distance. Just as I was passing the temple, I heard a commotion and shouting inside. I moved to see what was happening, convinced it would be officials arguing about Yeshua.

It wasn't. Instead, I heard a voice that made me freeze.

It was Yudah. Clear as day. I moved closer to see what was going on.

He was just inside the main doors with people I didn't recognise.

'I've done wrong,' he was shouting now, in a frenzy. He was holding his head in his hands and tearing at his hair. 'I've betrayed an innocent man!'

A disinterested official was trying to get him to leave the temple area.

'What do I care? That's your problem!'

Then I saw Yudah reach inside his cloak and pull out a bag of coins. He threw them at the official. The coins scattered across the stone floor, and I saw Yudah turn and burst out of the temple at a sprint.

I quickly followed, assuming that Yudah was going to follow the mob to Pilate's residence. But after a few moments, he turned the other way. And he kept running. Faster and faster.

I raced after him as best I could.

He was screaming out loud as he tore down the alleyways, then out through one of the city gates. I couldn't keep up with him, and I stumbled and fell more than once.

I lost him as he raced out into the fields beyond. Some time later I found him, but the deed was already done.

Yudah had tied a length of rope to a branch, then roughly around his neck, and had hung himself.

His lifeless body was gently swinging beneath the tree.

I stood where I was. Listening to the birdsong that marked the start of the day.

78

Judgement (Friday)

THERE WAS ONLY one place I wanted to go, and I hurried there as fast as I could. By the time I arrived, the crowd of onlookers was hundreds deep outside the gates of Pilate's palace.

They were all fighting for a view, and the rumour mill about what was going on inside was in overdrive.

I put my hood up and slipped in among them. I was careful to stay well back from where the chief priest and his religious advisors were standing together at the front. I tried to piece together what had happened by listening to the chatter.

Apparently, the chief priest had hoped he could just hand the Master over to the Romans, tell them that he was a trouble-maker, and leave them to do the rest. But it hadn't proved that easy. Pilate had been less than impressed when the chief priest turned up at such an early hour demanding action.

At first, nothing happened, but eventually, there was a flash of movement on the other side of the gates and the Roman compound opened. Pilate himself then emerged onto the raised steps at the front of the colonnade.

Soldiers were everywhere throughout the palace courtyard. And on the steps, eight guards flanked the battered, bruised and tightly bound Master. The blindfold was now gone from his head, and Yeshua seemed able to stand on his own – though the bruising and blood was clear to see.

One eye was completely closed over with swelling.

The moment I saw him, my heart started to race.

I wanted to shout out that he was innocent. That this man deserved to be set free. That he was the light of the world. God himself made man.

Could they not see it? Did they not know? Had they not seen his works?

I kept silent, partly out of fear, but partly because I knew, even then, that this was part of the Master's plan. He had forewarned us many times of what would happen. Of these events. Even if we had never wanted to believe it.

Yeshua stood tied and bound by Roman guards, as Pilate addressed him for what felt like an age. There was a low rumble in the crowd as they watched in anticipation at the verdict.

Then Pilate raised his hand to silence the crowd and started to speak.

'You brought this man to me. You said he was trying to change the people, but I judged him before you all and have not found him guilty of the things you say he has done.' Pilate paused, as if he was tired of the discussion.

'Look, he has done nothing bad enough for the death penalty.'

The crowd erupted with shouts of accusation. But it was impossible to hear them. It was clear to us all, and to Pilate, that Yeshua had been handed over because of the Pharisees' fears and jealousy. But it appeared the accusations weren't sticking.

While Pilate was standing there in the place of judgement, a Roman centurion then approached him with a small scroll.

We later heard from some of those who worked within Pilate's household that it was a handwritten note from Pilate's wife. It simply read: 'Don't do anything with that man. He is not guilty. Last night I had a dream about him, and it troubled me very much . . .'

But we didn't know of this until much later.

Pilate then stepped forward, threw his arm wide towards the Master, and called out in a voice that rang with annoyance.

'Look at this man. I find nothing wrong in him.'

To Pilate, the Master certainly did not look like the dangerous man that many had made him out to be.

My heart started beating even faster. Hope flooded in.

'Maybe this had been the plan all along? Was the Master about to be released, his death spared, just like Isaac's was at the last moment from his father Abraham?'

At the same time, the crowd surged forward. I was sure

that many of those gathered would have been among those who had happily welcomed Yeshua into the city only five days earlier. They loved what Yeshua had said; what he had done.

I was convinced that the crowd would demand his release.

Many in the city were wise to the lies and manipulations that the priests were capable of. Protecting themselves at all costs.

Pilate then directed the next question straight at Yeshua.

'So tell me, are You a king then?'

Pilate's words were laden with meaning and everyone around looked at Yeshua intently for his response.

Yeshua lifted his head.

'You say rightly that I am a king.' The words came out calmly and quietly.

'For this I was born and for this I came into the world. To testify to the truth. Everyone who belongs to the truth listens to my voice.'

At this the murmuring in the crowd started up again.

The priests bristled and tensed. They had their own soldiers around them, and they were glaring out at the crowd, as if preparing to single people out if they fell out of line. Pilate's eyes moved from the crowd to the priests. He was speaking to them now.

'It's your custom that I pardon one prisoner at Passover. Do you want me to pardon this so-called "King"?'

It was a clever compromise solution.

But almost at once, the priests and their heavies started up a chant, calling for Barabbas, the murderer and rebel, to be released instead.

The crowd laughed.

As if that could be called any sort of genuine choice.

Barabbas, the killer, against this poor, beaten Galilean stonemason and teacher. They were chalk and cheese. And everyone knew it.

Yet somehow the cries of 'Barabbas' were starting to spread.

It made no sense to me.

Then I spotted the priests and their officials, riling and

encouraging the crowd. Urging them, coercing them, to chant the word 'Barabbas'.

Pilate listened a while, then shook his head in despair. As if acknowledging that he would never truly fathom the minds of these defeated Israelites.

He waved his hand, silenced the crowd and announced that he was done – they could have their rebel Barabbas. And as for this peasant man before him? He would order him flogged and scourged, if that's what they wanted. Let that suffice.

With that, Pilate turned on his heels and left the colonnade.

The rest of us watched as the Master was dragged away.

79

Flog, Flay, Scourge (Friday)

THE PRIESTS STILL weren't satisfied though, and the small crowd of hecklers kept chanting.

Even though the Roman 'flog and scourge' was notorious for ripping most of the skin and flesh from the human body, it seemed such a punishment still wouldn't be enough for those who wanted Yeshua dead. But Pilate ignored their chants and was gone.

There was nothing for any of us to do but wait.

Within minutes, I heard the whipping start.

Even from the front of the palace, the sound was unmistakable. Obscured behind the closed gates of the inner courtyard, the crack and hiss of the whip slicing through the air was agony to listen to.

Then the muffled cries and screams. I covered my ears. The brutal sound of flesh being torn from bone. Each crack now ending with the cry of pain.

Such agony was impossible to stay contained.

Again, and again. That crack. I lost count of how many times he was being whipped.

Life being stripped and beaten out of him. Literally.

Soon I could hear the cries no more. Yet the whipping continued.

I feared the worst.

A Roman scourging whip was a fearsome instrument of torture. Designed to induce pain and compliance in the extreme. The whip itself was laced with small metal balls and spikes. Its purpose was to flay the human body of all flesh, skin, dignity and resistance.

I knew that victims routinely died at the hands of a Roman

scourging. It was designed to break the human spirit and take victims to the very edge of life and death.

Few survived it.

When it was finally over, and the whip fell silent, a cold, spent sensation fell on us all in the crowd.

Then Pilate came out again, and the crowd gasped. At first, I didn't recognise the figure that the guards were dragging in between them. Apart from a purple cloak on his shoulders and a blood-soaked cloth around his waist, he was naked.

His flesh was bright red. There was barely any skin left untouched across his entire body. This hadn't just been some sort of minor infringement whipping; it had been a flaying in the extreme.

Blood was seeping down his whole carcass, pooling on the white stone at his feet. He was barely able to stand and was supported between two guards. On his head was a twisted band of heavy thorns, forced down through the skin.

I felt myself stagger and stumble backwards. I wanted to wretch.

Oh, my Master, what have you allowed to be done?

80

No King But Caesar (Friday)

I COULDN'T UNDERSTAND IT.

I'd seen the Master raise Elazar from the dead and I'd witnessed the heavens open. I'd seen him walk on water and calm the storm. Surely, if he wanted to walk free, no soldier on earth could hold him?

Yet he chooses this?

It was beyond what I could comprehend.

Pilate then slowly stepped forward, so that he was beside the broken figure of Yeshua.

'I present him to you. Are you happy now?'

He paused.

'I want you to know that I do not find him guilty of any crime worthy of death.'

He then turned towards Yeshua, and the soldiers shoved the Master forward. He staggered and fell. I could see even more clearly now how badly he had been flogged. Muscle, bone and tissue bleeding and exposed.

Pilate's voice was laced with sarcasm now.

'Here he is: the King of the Jews.'

At this, the high priest himself shouted out loud, 'We have no king but Caesar . . .'

It was a genius retort. And Pilate felt it.

It stopped him in his tracks.

Then the crowd started screaming out, 'Crucify! Crucify!'

Pilate held his ground, then shook his head.

He wasn't going to be coerced.

'You take him,' he yelled back, as if this was a private conversation just between him and the chief priest.

'You crucify him. I find nothing wrong with him.'

One of the other priests then shouted out, 'We have a law.

228

And by that law he must die because he claimed to be the Son of God.'

Pilate looked piqued. This conversation had already gone on long enough.

He walked right up to where Yeshua lay and told the guards to get him to his feet.

Then he addressed the Master. 'Where did you come from?'

The Master said nothing.

'You won't talk? Don't you know that I have the authority to pardon you, and the authority to crucify you?'

The Master tried to speak. It was hard for him to form the words, his mouth swollen and broken. But through the spit and blood, he fought to get the words out clearly.

'You haven't a shred of authority over me . . . except what has been given you from heaven . . .'

Pilate smiled despairingly.

The crowds continued to chant. 'Crucify! Crucify!'

Pilate turned back to the crowd, his hands held up, head shaking.

'I am to crucify your king?'

The high priest turned and waved his arm, deferring to the crowd sarcastically. Their chants were his answer.

The message was clear: *If you want to avoid trouble today, give us what we demand.*

The crowd had spoken.

Pilate shrugged his shoulders, then he went and washed his hands in the large gold bowl that stood beside him.

'I am not guilty of this man's death. You are the ones who are doing it!'

One of the religious elite in the crowd shouted back, 'We will take full responsibility for his death. You can blame us!'

Enough was enough.

Pilate nodded to the guards and left.

The Master was going to be crucified.

81

The Place of the Skull (Friday)

THE JOURNEY TO the Place of the Skull was almost half a mile, but it took longer than I ever thought possible.

The Master was barely able to stand, but the guards forced him to carry the cross beam which was strapped with rough rope across his bleeding shoulders.

The wooden beam was not far off the weight of a man. The Master would struggle to take a few steps, then stumble or trip under the weight and collapse.

The guards would then beat him to his feet and urge him onwards, with shouts and whips and taunts.

Nobody dared step forward to help him.

Where is my neighbour?

The crowds were pressing in on every side. The priests continued to shout at whoever would listen, that Pilate had ruled the Galilean a blasphemer who deserved to die.

Many were shouting abuse at the Master.

'Blasphemer!'

Others spat or threw things at him as he staggered past and up the long hill.

The same streets the Master had walked before, but now the cries of 'Hosanna' were gone, drowned out by hate.

It was mid-morning now and the sun was starting to get hot. When the Master had covered less than a quarter of the distance, he took one final fall and could then move no more. No matter how much they kicked, beat and coerced him, he was barely able to crawl.

The soldiers then pulled a random man out of the crowd. He looked terrified, but they forced him to help Yeshua carry the wooden beam.

I then noticed the Master's mother in the crowd, and with

her was Myriam of Magdala. Both hidden under shawls and weeping out loud. I went to them and held them, and together we stumbled on behind the Master as he edged his way up towards the Place of the Skull.

The crowds were thinning out now, as we got further from the city streets, and soon we managed to get within sight of the Master.

At one point, he collapsed again, and he spotted us as he looked up from the dusty ground. His eyes were encrusted with blood and dirt and his mouth ripped and barely able to open.

He nodded at us. Slowly.

'Don't cry for me,' he muttered with broken words. 'Cry for yourselves and for your children.' He took a laboured breath. 'The time is coming when they'll say, "Lucky the women who never conceived! Lucky the wombs that never gave birth!"'

Yeshua then continued, staggering towards the place where the Romans routinely execute criminals in the most cruel, painful and humiliating way imaginable, and our tiny hope vanished.

When the Master finally made it to the Place of the Skull, the soldiers wasted no time.

Yeshua collapsed on the ground, his blood oozing into the dust. The soldiers barely gave this 'criminal' a second glance. They simply hauled him by his legs and dragged his broken body over to where the wooden post was now laid out on the ground.

Yeshua was lying face up in the dirt, looking to the sky. His eyes were wide open, and his body shook with fear for what was to come.

The soldiers roughly heaved Yeshua on top of the post and bolted the beam section to it, to form a cross.

82

Crucifixion (Friday)

THE SOLDIERS TIED a rope around one wrist and then wrapped it tight against the beam, so Yeshua's arm could not move. They then pulled him from the other side, forcing his arms agonisingly wide, until both wrists were bound tight against the cross. Yeshua cried out as they wrenched each arm to its limit.

Then came the nails.

Six inches long and half an inch wide, they were made of rough iron. One of the soldiers reached into a bucket and pulled several out. And a mallet hammer.

He then knelt on Yeshua's elbow and placed the nail crudely against Yeshua's palm.

Then the soldier lifted the mallet and drove the nail firmly through, between the bones and tendons.

One, two, three heavy blows from the weighted mallet, and then another long nail through his other hand, and they were in.

The Master was now pinned to the cross.

The nails through his hands went in relatively easy. The one holding both his feet in place against the rough wood was much tougher to get to bite.

The soldiers took many more blows to break through his feet. The cries from the Master were more desperate and agonised than anything I'd ever heard. Spit and phlegm bursting out of his broken lips and mouth.

Then I could see that Yeshua was trying to speak. Fighting to get words out of his beaten, swollen, bleeding lips.

Then I heard them. Mumbled at first, then louder.

'Father, forgive them.'

Each word was a struggle.

'Father, forgive them . . . they don't know what they're doing.'

The soldiers were doused in sweat after the exertion, but the first part of their job was done.

The Master was locked in. Nailed to his cross.

Blood was pouring from his wounds.

The pain got even worse for the Master as they heaved the cross upright, and his weight began to sag onto his hands and feet. He let out a prolonged howl of agony.

When the cross dropped into the base that held it in position, it did so with a violent thud, and the shock echoed through the Master's body as now his entire weight fell onto his pinned limbs.

He screamed out loud with all his voice and might. Instantly, he was struggling to breathe. His chest was being pulled upwards by his splayed arms, while the weight of the rest of his body was pulling him down. Just to get a small amount of air into his lungs was taking a herculean effort against gravity and extreme pain.

Excruciating. It is where the very word had come from. *Ex. Cruciate.* Out of the cross . . . comes pain that the Romans had made unbearable.

It was no accident that across the Roman Empire, the threat of public crucifixion had become their method of spreading terror and compliance into conquered people. To be crucified was to be broken – reserved for killing slaves or the worst criminals.

And the agony could last for hours. Days sometimes.

All Yeshua's bodyweight was now hanging on the three bolts nailed through his hands and feet. Every breath requiring him to haul his body up to take the weight off his chest. But to haul himself up meant intense pain as all his weight came onto his pierced feet.

Crucifixion meant to die from the long agony of torn tendons and nerves and the slow torture of suffocation.

Not that the soldiers cared. They just mocked the Master as he hung there.

As Pilate had instructed them, one of the soldiers then bolted a rough block of wood onto the cross itself. On it were crudely carved the words:

'YESHUA OF NAZARET. KING OF THE JEWS.'

They all then stood back and laughed.

83

The Thief (Friday)

I STOOD NEARBY with Myriam, the Master's mother, as well as the other Myriam, from Magdala. A few of the other women disciples were also with us. We longed to be able to hold and support Yeshua, but the soldiers wouldn't let us get any closer than we were.

To hear his cries of visceral pain was crushing. Powerless to help the Master in his greatest hour of need. Again.

Many others stood around watching as well – some with tears, some with hate and mockery, some out of morbid fascination. The Romans certainly knew how to put on a show of horror and intimidation.

Many were there out of intrigue. After all, this man – hanging, bleeding, dying – had claimed to be the Son of God. If ever there was a time to show your proof, it should be now.

The soldiers knew it too.

Some of them even started throwing dice to decide who would keep the Master's bloodied undergarment that he had been wearing.

Yeshua was watching the soldiers through the one blood-encrusted eyelid that held open. Yet there was not a hint of hate in his eye.

Some spectators started jeering at him.

'You bragged that you could tear down the temple and then rebuild it in three days. So? Go on! Show us your power!'

They laughed, then spat at him and walked on.

One of the chief priests stood there and challenged him:

'Save yourself. If you're really God's Son, come down from that cross. We are all watching. Waiting!'

Kaiaphas, the high priest, didn't even care to be there to see his work. But others among the priests came. Some weren't content just to watch the crucifixion – the torture and nailing of the man to the wood. That wasn't enough, it seemed.

They wanted to mock him.

He saved others but it seems he can't save himself! King of Israel? Then come down from the cross and we will all believe . . .

There were two other men crucified with the Master that day. Two criminals. Thieves. One on the left of him, the other on the right. The three crosses made for a haunting, terrifying sight against the skyline of Yerushalayim behind.

The Place of the Skull indeed was a place of death – but it was also a place of horror. Outside of the city, it had become the place the Romans chose to exercise their brutality and to make it visible to the masses. High on a hill, a place where all could see.

And behind the torture site was a pit of dust, dirt and rotting corpses.

Criminals cut down from the cross rotted close by to where they died. The smell alone was a reminder that Roman rule is undeniable.

One of the criminals on Yeshua's left started mocking him too, as he hung on his cross, bleeding and suffocating in agony.

Through agonised breaths, the criminal challenged the Master to save himself, and the two of them while he was at it. He spat out the words and then dropped his head again as he tried to breathe.

But the other criminal spoke out in a loud voice in the Master's defence.

'Have you no fear of God?' he shouted to the mocker. Then he was silent for a few moments, as he fought the asphyxiation and pain. Then he continued in a low voice, 'We deserve this, but not him. He did nothing wrong.'

In broken words, the same thief lifted and turned his bleeding head towards the Master and mumbled the words, 'Remember me when you enter your kingdom.'

The Master at first was silent.

Then I saw him turn his head slowly to the thief beside him. The Master tried to talk, but no words came out. He took in a laboured, pained breath. Words were agonising to come by.

Finally, Yeshua muttered through the blood, spit and dust.

'I promise you, today you will be with me in paradise.'

84

The Final Breath (Friday)

AS THE MORNING wore on, slowly, the crowds drifted away.

I didn't know how long the Master could survive up there. I just wished it could be over quickly now. The heartbreak of watching him die like this was unbearable.

He was growing weaker with every breath. Yet the pain never seemed to diminish.

While the soldiers were standing around organising themselves, roughly tidying away their instruments of execution, Yeshua's mother, Myriam, remained silently weeping at the foot of the cross. Powerless to do anything for Yeshua as he hung in agony above her. Her eyes were red with pain and anguish.

At one point, Yeshua turned his head and looked straight at me, then back to his mother. He mumbled through parched lips: 'Woman, here is your son.' Then to me, he simply whispered, 'Here is your mother.'

From that moment I knew the end was close.

Even though it was almost midday, I suddenly noticed that the sky was growing darker. Thick, black clouds were rolling in, and within a few minutes all daylight was replaced by a terrifying darkness.

We looked at each other. We had no idea what was happening.

Just as the sky was darkening so dramatically, a bitter wind also blew in. Yeshua was starting to writhe in even more pain now. Moaning out loud with every laboured heave of his chest. His face was contorted with agony, his head thrashing from side to side.

Then suddenly, the Master screamed out loud, in a voice that was wrought with raw pain and terror, 'My God, my God, why have you abandoned me?'

The very words from the vision that the psalmist King David had seen so many centuries earlier. The fate of the Messiah. Total abandonment.

Yeshua's cry was of raw dereliction. We stood and wept. Powerless to help.

The minutes passed now like years. The sky remained eerily dark. We sat there, holding each other, staring up at the man we loved.

The soldiers left us alone; they were bored, waiting for their murderous task to be completed. Almost all the spectators had now gone. It was just us, waiting, praying for death to come.

Then the Master whispered out loud, 'I'm . . . thirsty.' His voice was cracked and broken.

The soldiers didn't even bother to stop us as we soaked a sponge in some wine and water then placed it on the end of a stick and held it up to the Master to drink.

He barely took a sip, then his head dropped down on his chest, and in one laboured gasp and desperate heave of his chest, he let out a broken cry:

'It is finished!'

A low, mighty rumble ripped through the air around us. Then the rocks beneath us started to tremble. I had never experienced anything like this. All of us stood there were thrown to the ground.

We shook in terror at what was happening. The earth itself seemed to be groaning. Grieving, even. Time. Space. History. All coming together; all coming down to this one spot. On a small, dusty hill outside the city.

We later heard that at that very same moment, something incredible had happened in the temple. Right there, in the place where the Master had taught, loved, argued and healed, the giant temple curtain that guarded the inner holy sanctum, the place where only the most chosen of priests could ever enter, was torn in two, from top to bottom. As if someone had ripped it open.

The great temple curtain, as high as ten men, and as thick as a man's hand, the very symbol that always appeared to separate the ordinary people from God, was split in half. The barrier between us and the Almighty was gone.

Up at the Place of the Skull, the darkness was still all-consuming.

The Master twisted and pushed against the nails, filling his lungs one more time as pain shot through his body.

'Father,' he yelled out, each word agonised and laboured, 'I place my life in your hands . . .'

His head fell forward one last time. Then his body visibly dropped and sagged, the weight hanging against the iron bolts.

The Master was dead.

Then suddenly, one of the Roman centurions who had been administering the punishment, the man who had handled the nails, spear, beating and crucifixion, slowly dropped to his knees.

He had witnessed Yeshua's torment and seen his forgiveness of the thief on the cross beside him; he had seen the sky turn black and the earth shake before him.

The soldier spoke out quiet words that no Roman guard had ever said before:

'Truly, this man was the Son of God.'

PART FIVE

Myriam of Magdala

MAGDALA
c. AD 33

A bustling fishing port on the shores of the Sea of Galilee.

85

Set Free

AROUND 3 YEARS EARLIER.

EVEN TODAY, IF I close my eyes, I can remember the first time I met Yeshua. I was only nineteen.

I remember it because it was the first time in my life that I had felt a physical force of power and strength suddenly fill my body. And I had most definitely never experienced that before.

For as long as I could remember, I had struggled with my health.

On the surface, you would not have known. I'd been able to walk, talk, even play at times. And on the days I felt strong enough, I was able to carry out chores and tasks at home.

But I didn't feel that strength very often.

I grew scared that I would never be well enough to live a normal life. Never be able to marry, be a mother, or simply ever be able to live my life as I had dreamt of when I was a child.

Inside, I was in turmoil. My days and nights were a constant tornado of fear and sorrow that would rarely let me go. Even on a good day, I could feel those forces lurking, waiting for me. And they would always return.

One moment, I could be gripped by a terrifying panic that made my heart race and my skin sweat. Minutes later, I could be plunged into a despair so bleak that I hoped only for death.

And I hated myself for such thoughts.

Why could I not be normal?

I could talk to no one. Because no one would understand.

I had spent all my teenage years living like this. Yet, I had prayed and prayed that when I became an adult, the fear and shame would pass.

Instead, it got worse. And the more I disguised it, the more I denied it, the darker and more controlling a presence it became in my life.

My family knew that all was not well. I told them I felt weak and tired a lot of the time. But the physical weakness was only a small part of the deeper issue. The truth I could not share.

My family were well-meaning. They talked to several doctors. Even a priest. They even took me to a supposed wise woman who had once travelled all the way to Rome and brought back strange herbs which she brewed and sold. The potion tasted foul and did not help me at all.

I pretended to my family that it did.

So I would hide. Smile. Breathe. Pray that the panic, the fear and the despair would not return. But it always did.

And it was always worse at night.

Alone can be an awful place to be.

And then by daybreak, I would be exhausted. And I would look it.

All of this made me 'unusual' to everyone else my age. And unusual is rarely popular.

Not that I cared too much.

I had more important things to worry about. Like the night ahead.

And that was my world: Fear. Panic. Then pain. Then shame.

That was until the day that Yeshua came to my village.

I don't know how I ended up in front of him. The man I would come to know and love as my Lord. I don't know what transpired that suddenly I was in front of him. Facing him. Alone. But somehow, not afraid.

But I do remember what he said.

'Myriam.'

His voice was warm. Gentle. It spoke right to me.

His voice didn't just go into my head. It travelled straight into my heart.

And with that voice, my fear melted away.

It was as if when he spoke the sound of my name, it was waking something within me that had been buried for years.

I remember looking into his face. So full of light.

Then he spoke simple words that released me.

I was free. And at once everything changed. I could feel again.

I could hear the birds outside.

All that panic, shame and fear just lifted off me. Like one of those birds. As if they had taken flight and simply flown away. There was no more weight on my chest, no more choking breath. Instead, there was life. There was hope.

And there was pure love.

I knew right then that I would spend the rest of my life following this man who had set me free.

My Lord.

86

Unbridled Grief (Saturday)

THE DAY I watched my Lord being tortured, whipped, then executed, had been the worst day of my life.

The sun finally set, and my heart was broken and empty. I had no more tears to cry.

That evening, one of our group, Yosef, from the town of Arimathea, went to see Pilate privately. Yosef was a man of influence with the Romans, a respected and wealthy merchant as well. But he was also a quiet follower and admirer of Yeshua. We knew him relatively well.

Yosef had respectfully asked Pilate to allow him formally to bury Yeshua's body. Pilate had agreed and given orders for the soldiers discreetly to hand over the body to the wealthy merchant.

From the Place of the Skull, Yosef organised for the body to be carried down to a small cave tomb that he had purchased at significant expense.

I had watched as Yosef arranged for Yeshua to be wrapped in a new linen cloth and placed carefully inside the cold tomb.

Then, with the help of some friends, a huge stone was rolled across the entrance.

That was it – sealed and done.

My heart broke once more.

I was so grateful to Yosef, and so relieved it was over now. That my Lord could lie in peace. Finally, at rest. That he was being given the respect and dignity his life and death so deserved.

After Yosef had organised all this, he placed a hand on my shoulder and offered his final condolences. Then he smiled gently, turned into the night and headed home.

I was left sitting near the tomb as night descended.

I did not know where else to go.

I just wanted to be close to my Lord. Even in death.

I fell asleep where I sat, curled up in a blanket against the bitter cold.

Early the next day, soldiers mounted guard in the garden, watching the tomb and taking shifts.

Apparently, the leading priests and the Pharisees had beseeched Pilate to do this, saying, 'Sir, we remember that while that liar was still alive, he said, "I will rise from death in three days." So, give the order for the tomb to be guarded well for three days, or his followers might come and try to steal the body. Then they could tell everyone that he has risen from death. That lie will be even worse than what they said about him before.'

Pilate had understood and agreed to the request. The last thing he wanted was more trouble. The body would be guarded, and there would be no doubt as to the finality and death of the renegade Yeshua.

After all, Yeshua's death had been all anyone had talked about in the city since yesterday. And people were hungry for the story to continue. A missing or stolen body would do exactly that.

It is why I was relieved to see soldiers sent to guard the tomb of my Lord.

I sat in that garden all that day. I ate nothing. I just lay on the ground and mourned.

Each minute passing felt like time was taking me further and further from my Lord. The gulf was growing between us. I was alone. And for the first time since I had met Yeshua, I was afraid. All over again.

The stone was heavy, the guards menacing and the tomb forbidding. Yeshua's body would soon begin to decompose.

The very thought broke my heart.

87

The Rock (Sunday)

I DON'T KNOW at what point I fell asleep on that second night. But in the early dawn when I awoke and returned to the tomb, I instantly noticed something was wrong.

The soldiers were now gone. Nowhere to be seen.

That seemed strange to me. I went up to investigate.

It was then that I noticed that the huge rock had been rolled away from the entrance.

My heart was instantly racing.

I had watched that rock being manhandled into position by several men only a day earlier. Yet now it had somehow been rolled away without so much as a scuffle.

I was confused. I had seen or heard nothing.

I stood there, motionless. Unsure what to do.

I then peeped inside the cold tomb cave and saw that my Lord's body was missing.

It was at that point that I panicked.

All I could think was go and find Kephas and Yohanan. Tell them. They would know what to do.

I didn't want to wake the others or to distress Myriam, Yeshua's mother. If she discovered that Yeshua's body was now missing, I did not know if she would be able to bear the heartache all over again.

I was determined that she should not be woken until we had discovered the truth.

I just needed Kephas and Yohanan to come and see for themselves. They might know something that I did not.

It was still dark when I raised them from their sleep, but they followed me at once.

We moved quickly, and in no time we were in the garden again. The two men cautiously approached the tomb.

Just as I had told them, the stone had been moved away. The soldiers were still nowhere to be found and the cave was wide open.

The body of Yeshua was gone.

As the two men exited the tomb, Kephas grabbed Yohanan by the tunic with a wild look of panic in his eyes.

'Who has done this?'

Then he turned to me.

'You were here all night, Myriam. Who came here and did this?'

'I saw nothing. I awoke and the guards were gone, the rock moved and the body missing!'

The two men stared at me, then at each other. They were as confused as I was.

Then Yohanan announced, 'Whoever has done this, the first thing is that we must tell the others.'

And with that, they turned and started to hurry back out of the garden.

88

The Folded Shroud (Sunday)

I WAS ALONE now. Stood there, uncertain about what I should do.

I nervously gathered my shawl in my arms. Part of me wanted to go back into the tomb. To check once again.

Were we all going mad?

But I knew what I had seen. The tomb had been empty. Yet I had to double-check.

I started back towards the cave, and slowly ventured inside.

I was calmer this time.

I'd been in tombs before. My own father's and a few others. There had always been a sense of decay and cold death. It never leaves you.

The air in Yeshua's though, felt somehow different. It was still cold and dark, but there was no feel of death inside. I remember that surprising me.

Nor was there the usual smell of human decomposition that you'd expect after three days. If I hadn't known better, I'd have said that the tomb had been empty for months.

I pushed a little further inside the tomb.

In a few moments, my eyes adjusted better to the darkness. And I could make out the shelf where the body had been. It was indeed empty. The body gone. Just as I had seen before.

But then I noticed something unusual that I hadn't seen when I had first peeped in. The linen burial shroud that Yeshua had been wrapped in was neatly folded and placed at the end of the shelf.

It didn't make sense.

If you're stealing a body from a tomb, why leave the linen shroud?

And why go to the trouble of folding it?

I looked around the cave for anything else of note. But there was nothing.

So I got ready to leave. I turned my back to the empty shelf and started to take a step when I noticed something out of the corner of my eye.

I looked back round. Then gasped out loud.

89

'Why Do You Weep?'

THE FIGURES WERE in the exact spot where the body of Yeshua had lain. Sat peacefully on the empty shelf.

But the shelf was no longer empty.

Faces radiant, light emanating from their bodies, were two brightly lit angels. And they were smiling at me. It looked as if heaven was bursting out of them. The light so consuming.

The sight of them took my breath away . . .

I just stood there, frozen to the spot, staring at the two angels. I was in shock.

One of the angels then turned directly to me and said, 'Why do you weep?'

My voice was quivering with fear. I could hear myself, but I sounded like I was outside of myself.

'They took my Master,' my voice just a whisper, 'and I don't know where they put him.'

I had a thousand questions for the angels, but I never got to ask them, because at that moment I heard footsteps behind me. I was suddenly aware that there was someone else there.

I turned and looked back at the tomb entrance. A man was standing in the opening. It was hard to see him clearly as he was silhouetted by the first rays of daylight spilling in behind him.

'Why do you weep?' he asked. 'Who are you looking for?'

I did not recognise the voice, and for some reason that I'll never quite understand, I got the idea in my head that this man was the gardener. I was worried that he would ask what I was doing in there.

In a moment of confusion and fear, I stumbled out the words, 'Sir, if you took him, tell me where you put him so I can care for him.'

The man stood silent.

Heaven seemed to hold its breath.

And then he spoke again.

And it was now that I recognised him.

'Myriam.'

That voice.

It was all I needed to hear.

The voice that I could not mistake. The voice I had first heard years earlier in my time of illness and despair.

The voice that I feared I had lost forever.

I leapt up and screamed, 'My Lord!'

I ran to him.

But before I could embrace him as I would have done before, he stopped me.

'Do not hold on to me.' He smiled.

And in that moment, I knew something new had begun.

'Do not be afraid.' He spoke softly. 'Go instead to my brothers and tell them . . .'

90

Heads Made of Cloth

THERE WAS NO doubting what I had seen.

It had been him. Yeshua. I had seen my Lord.

He had spoken to me out loud. Said my name. So beautifully.

Then he had disappeared again from my sight.

I ran, even though my feet kept on getting stabbed against stones. I ran so fast that my lungs burned, and I wanted to stop and gasp for more air, but I kept on running.

I had to tell the others.

After two days of weeping and grieving, then finding the tomb empty and all the confusion of that, now at last I knew.

Now I understood.

I had seen the Lord alive.

The sun was just starting to peek above the distant horizon. And as I sprinted from the garden to the house where the followers were staying, I kept thinking how I would tell them.

Tell them what I'd discovered. That the tomb was empty for a reason.

The body wasn't missing or stolen. It was simply happening as Yeshua had foretold.

I wondered to myself why I had ever expected anything else.

As I ran though, I had a niggling fear in my heart.

Would they believe me?

I already knew the answer.

You've seen him? Alive? Stop being hysterical.

I could hear it now.

When I finally made it to the house, I banged loudly on the locked door, panting for breath.

Without Yeshua beside them, the men had been fearing for their safety for over three days now. The city was a divided place and it had become dangerous to be associated with a crucified criminal.

Especially this one.

So, the followers kept the door firmly bolted.

When they cautiously opened the door, I rushed in. No stealth was needed this time. I had great news.

Kephas and Yohanan were already inside, talking animatedly to Andreas, Yakov and the others. All of us had barely slept since Passover, and the men looked sallow and tired. The news of the empty tomb was even more worrying to them.

'What is it, Myriam?' said Kephas as I stood there trying to catch my breath.

I tried to compose myself, but I couldn't hold it in a second longer.

I just blurted it out.

'I've seen him! He's alive!'

The men stared at me like I was mad.

'Stop all this,' Yakov said. 'What are you even talking about?'

I took some deep breaths, wiped the tears from my face and tried again.

'The Master's no longer dead. Our Lord. I spoke to him!'

They looked at me wearily.

I said it again: 'He's alive and well! Just after you left. He appeared. I thought at first he was the gardener, but it wasn't. It was him!'

The men looked at me then at each other, unsure how to respond. Then it came. The response and tone I had dreaded.

'Myriam, you're tired,' Yakov said to me. 'The tomb might be empty, Yohanan and Kephas have told us, but Yeshua isn't alive and well, I can assure you.'

That made me furious.

'No! You're not listening. Why won't you believe me?' I was shouting at them now. 'Are your heads made of cloth? I'm telling you the truth! I swear it!'

But it was no use. I couldn't do anything that would convince them.

They would not budge. And they did not want Myriam, Yeshua's mother, to hear of this sort of talk.

To them, I was simply talking nonsense.

After all, I was a woman, and the testimony of a woman in matters of life and death, court and justice are not even considered.

I was arguably the worst person that the Lord could have appeared to. But such was his way. Yeshua always cared more about love and truth than convincing anyone of anything.

He'd once told us if we had faith the size of a mustard seed, we could tell that mountain to move from here to there and it would.

He had told us that 'Nothing will be impossible for you.'

I had to trust that.

And that the time would come when he would appear again.

91

'He Cannot Be Alive!'

THERE WAS ANOTHER knock at the door.

Instantly, the men tensed up. The knock turned out to be Clopas and his companion, and they too were bursting with excitement. Both looked just as shocked and emboldened as I was.

I knew at once that they too had seen the Lord!

They quickly told us what had happened.

How they'd met a traveller on the road out of the city. They hadn't been able to see his face properly. But he had started talking to them about how the Scriptures had foretold the Messiah, and the man later broke bread and shared food with them. Then they realised who it was.

It wasn't just some random traveller. It was Yeshua himself. But as fast as he had come along beside them, he had then disappeared.

I smiled and looked around expectantly.

I now knew with even more certainty that this was all real – because it felt like Yeshua was toying with us. It was as if he was somehow enjoying these encounters. Such was the Lord's way. That sense of fun. It was part of what made him so beautiful to be around.

I looked at the other followers for their response.

Would they believe me now?

But still they refused.

They dismissed the three of us as deluded. In grief. They said we must have been seeing things. It was dark, after all.

And nothing that either Clopas or me could say would convince them.

Everyone understood that the body was gone. We had been hearing rumours all day that the guards charged with watching the tomb had fled when they saw the rock had been moved and the body missing.

Some even reported that the soldiers had been paid by the chief priests to spread rumours that we, the disciples, had stolen the body ourselves.

In short, everyone was confused.

But the one thing few believed was that Yeshua was alive.

92

'Peace Be with You'

WE WERE EATING all together when finally, it happened.

One moment it was just us, sitting around on the floor, talking. And then the next?

He was there.

The Lord. Yeshua himself. Standing right there in the middle of us all.

Nobody had opened the door. Nobody had undone the locks. But there he was, standing with his arms by his side, looking at each person in turn.

Smiling. As if he could hardly hold it in.

'Peace be with you,' he said, the light flickering in his eyes.

My heart leapt with delight.

'My Lord!'

The others, however, were speechless. Dumbfounded.

One even dropped his bowl on the floor.

They were terrified. As if they were seeing a ghost.

But Yeshua simply said, 'Why are you troubled? Why do you doubt what you see?'

He paused and looked at each of us in turn.

'Look at my hands and my feet. It's really me. Touch me. You can see that I have a living body; a ghost does not have a body like this.'

The followers could not believe what they were seeing in front of them.

Yeshua then said to them, 'Do you have any food here?'

That got them moving.

Andreas nervously gave Yeshua a piece of cooked fish, and we all watched as he took the fish and ate it.

Yeshua then said to them, 'Remember when I was with you before? I said that everything written about me must happen

– everything written in the law of Moses, the books of the prophets and the Psalms.'

We all nodded. Although I think most were still in a state of disbelief and shock.

Yeshua then closed his eyes as if to pray, and I copied. I breathed in deeply. A peace that words won't ever describe came over me.

And when I slowly opened my eyes, the Lord was gone.

93

'I Will Not Believe'

THE CHAOS THAT erupted was wild. People were laughing, and crying, hugging each other. Yakov even apologised to me. That was a first. Clopas just kept saying he had been trying to tell them.

Later that evening, Ta'om came back. As soon as he walked in, everyone was clambering to tell him the news, and what had happened.

But Ta'om wasn't convinced. He just refused to believe it.

'Unless I see the nail holes in his hands, put my finger in them and stick my hand in his side, I won't believe it. I saw him dead. Don't make this harder than it is already on yourselves.'

It took a week for it to happen again. We were back in the same house, and the followers remained paranoid about their safety. So, once again, the door was locked.

This time, all eleven of Yeshua's closest were with us, and when Yeshua appeared out of nowhere, just like he had before, it was Ta'om's turn for the blood to drain from his face.

Yeshua looked playfully at him. 'Peace be with you,' he said.

Ta'om slumped to his knees and his mouth dropped open.

I couldn't help but stifle a smile, at seeing Ta'om so utterly speechless.

Yeshua took a step towards him, his arms outstretched, palms upwards.

'Take your finger and examine my hands.'

He reached out towards Ta'om.

He turned his hands this way and that, revealing the deep wounds where the nails had gone through. The scars somehow looked like they had been part of him for his whole life.

It was the same with the gash in the side of his ribs.

After Yeshua had gasped his last on the cross, we had watched the soldiers move from cross to cross, criminal to criminal, to ensure each man was dead. The Romans don't like mistakes, especially when Shabbat is looming. What's to be done has to be done before the Shabbat holy day. All business to be completed. Even if that business is death.

We had watched as the soldiers had driven a spear into Yeshua's dead body. Right between his ribs and into his heart. Blood and fluid had drained out.

Yeshua spoke again to Ta'om.

'Take your hand and stick it in my side.'

He offered his side to Ta'om.

'Don't be unbelieving. Believe.'

As soon as he said those words, Ta'om started to weep.

'My Master!' he sobbed. 'My God.'

Yeshua then held Ta'om close into himself. He said nothing at all, just held Ta'om in a tight embrace and let him weep.

When his shoulders had finally stopped shaking, Yeshua spoke. His words were for us all.

'You believe because you've seen with your own eyes.'

He looked around at each of us and smiled.

'Even better blessings are in store for those who believe without seeing.'

94

Kephas' Cloak

I HADN'T BEEN there the night the disciples shared the Passover meal together, so I hadn't witnessed Yeshua tell Kephas that he would betray him three times before the night was over.

But I'd heard about it.

In the days between the crucifixion and Yeshua's return in the garden, there had been whispered conversations about what had happened. Some were shocked by his betrayal, others were more sympathetic.

But by the time Yeshua started appearing in front of us out of thin air, almost everyone had forgotten it.

All apart from Kephas.

He wore his shame like a cloak. It hid him and it weighed him down.

When Yeshua appeared to all of us on those first occasions, Kephas had hung back. Both times he had quietly retreated to the edge. Like a spider startled by the light. Safety was found in the shadows.

Both times, Yeshua had treated Kephas just like he did everyone else in the room. He looked at him with nothing but love and kindness. But it was clear that Kephas felt uncomfortable in his presence.

After all, he had gone from being the rock that Yeshua said he would build the future community of followers upon, to the man who betrayed him.

I am certain that was why Kephas decided so hastily to leave Yerushalayim and return to Galilee. He told us it was time to get back to work and start providing for his family once again. He wasn't the only one thinking it – three years away can feel a long time. He was joined by a handful of the others, including Ta'om, Yohanan and Yakov.

I was sad that they left so fast. And leaving Yerushalayim just didn't make sense to me. After all, Yeshua had made four separate appearances to his followers since his death, and they were all in or near the city. Yerushalayim appeared to be the epicentre for Yeshua.

If there was even the slimmest of chances that he'd show up again, why on earth would Kephas, Yohanan and the others risk missing it by heading back north?

But I was wrong.

95

Breakfast on the Beach

IT HAPPENED ONE day not long after Kephas and the others had moved back north.

Kephas had been feeling down for some days. Adrift, uncertain and still full of shame.

As was his way, he hoped that going fishing would help clear his heart and head.

It didn't.

All night, he and the others went around their old favourite spots, but they got nothing. It was as big a fishing failure as they could remember.

When the sun rose the next morning, they grudgingly decided to head back for home. Kephas' mood was even worse now, and they sailed in total silence.

Just when they were coming into the shore, they spotted someone standing on the beach ahead of them. He had a fire going and was calmly waving at the boat.

'Good morning!' yelled the stranger when they were close enough to hear. 'Did you catch anything for breakfast?'

'No,' growled Kephas, barely acknowledging the man.

The stranger carried on regardless. 'Throw the net off the right side of the boat and see what happens.' Kephas was swearing under his breath by now. The last thing Kephas needed was some idiot fishing enthusiast giving him advice.

But what had they to lose? The others casually did what the stranger suggested.

Suddenly, at the very moment they dropped them in, the nets became full to bursting. So full that the boat started to list to one side. So full that all six of those bad-tempered, weather-beaten fishermen, with arms like iron, couldn't haul the nets in.

They were shouting and hauling when Yohanan paused. He suddenly had a feeling about what was going on, and about this stranger on the beach.

So he stopped, covered his eyes against the sun and stared harder.

'Could it be . . .?' he said under his breath.

Then louder: 'It is . . . It's him! It's the Master!'

It was at that exact moment that something snapped within Kephas. And he didn't hold back like he had in Yerushalayim. Maybe it was because he was back in his old job, or maybe he'd just had enough of feeling shameful. Whatever the reason, he didn't stop to think. Instinct, as he was always telling us.

So, running on pure heart, Kephas grabbed his cloak and leapt over the side of the boat and swam, shouted and waded his way to shore.

Kephas rushed up to Yeshua, heaving for breath, and beaming with joy.

But then he stopped himself short.

Something needed to be said.

Kephas was trying to think how even to voice his regret when Yeshua, with a broad smile, told him, 'Bring me one of those fish you caught.'

Kephas was glad of the excuse and went back to the boat to help drag the nets ashore.

Meanwhile, Yeshua carried on tending the fire and the breakfast he had prepared. He had some bread ready, and soon, with the fresh fish they now had, the group were feasting and laughing like the old days.

As they finished this makeshift breakfast on the lake shore, Yeshua turned gently to Kephas, then he stood up and reached out his hand to his fisherman friend.

Yeshua beckoned Kephas to come and walk with him.

As they walked the shoreline, Yeshua turned to him.

'Kephas?' he said.

Still, Kephas kept his eyes low.

'Do you love me?'

'Yes, Master,' Kephas said, his voice barely a whisper. 'You know I love you.'

'Feed my lambs,' Yeshua replied.

Then, after a pause, he asked again: 'Do you love me?'

Kephas said it again: 'Yes, Master, you know I love you.'

Yeshua replied: 'Shepherd my sheep.'

The Master then asked a third, final time: 'Do you love me?'

Kephas was getting upset now with this repetition.

'Master,' he sighed, 'you know everything there is to know. You've got to know that I love you.'

Once more, Yeshua replied: 'Feed my sheep.'

And that was when it hit Kephas.

Three questions.

Yeshua was replacing those three denials – the source of Kephas' shame – with three words of restoration. Restoring him to his true place. The man on whom the future would be built.

The lambs, the sheep, that he was telling Kephas to feed and protect . . . they were the followers to come.

Then Yeshua placed his hand on Kephas' shoulder and smiled.

And the two men embraced and laughed like of old.

96

Until the End of Time

AFTER THAT MORNING on the beach, Kephas, Yohanan and the others made their way back to Yerushalayim. It was beautiful to see Kephas so free and alive once more.

The Lord continued to visit us, showing up at all hours of the night and day. We never had any warning, and we never knew when he was going to come. The only consistent things about his visits were that he never, ever, used the door. And that he was always hungry.

One minute, you'd be going about your business in the house – often it was when we were eating a meal together – then the next, there he would be. And he would always say, 'Peace be with you!' Then he'd start poking his head into whatever food we had around.

I think he enjoyed the fact that each mouthful he took in our presence was a reminder to us that he wasn't some sort of ghost or apparition.

The awkwardness of those first meetings had now vanished. And for weeks we carried on this way, him popping up unannounced then disappearing.

One time, he even appeared to over five hundred followers at the same time. It was mind-blowing for so many to experience. I saw the light and love of the Lord make broken hearts sing.

His presence was so beautiful – and it was unstoppable.

But somehow, I knew that his physical presence with us would not remain forever.

After all, what is faith if there is only certainty?

The next time he came, he did not eat, he just wanted to talk. There was an urgency now in his voice. I could feel my heart race as I listened.

'Go and make followers of all people in the world. Teach them to obey everything that I have told you to do. You can be sure that I will be with you always. I will continue with you until the end of time.'

I was so scared though to hear this. The idea of going anywhere without him was terrifying. But here he was telling us to go, to teach, to serve, to baptise. I felt so inadequate.

But then I remembered his words: 'I will be with you always.'

They were like breath upon the embers of a fire.

'I'll be with you.' It was all we needed.

I could feel my confidence start to build and my spirit ignite.

97

The Beginning . . .

WHEN FORTY DAYS had passed since he first appeared in the garden, Yeshua made his final appearance to us.

One moment we were alone, then there he was among us, again.

He said nothing about this being the last physical visitation that he would make.

With hindsight, I should have known.

He led us out of the house, down through the city gates and along the valley, up beyond Gad Smane and into the hills towards Beth 'Anya. The journey we had done so many times together.

When we reached the top of this small hill, called Tura Zita, the Mount of Olives, Yeshua turned and stopped.

He reached out his hands to us and held on tight to each of us in turn.

Andreas asked him, 'Master, are you going to restore your kingdom now? Is this the time?'

Yeshua told them that God's own Spirit would come to them. 'Dates and times. They are not for you to know. But the Holy Spirit will come upon you and give you power. You will be my witnesses. You will tell people everywhere about me – in Yerushalayim, in the rest of Yehuda, in Samaria, and in every part of the world.'

His arms were now raised above him, and his eyes closed. His head lifted up to the heavens.

Suddenly, the light around him started to change. And a brightness began to shine out from him. A brightness that was almost impossible to look at.

Then a cloud began to form around him. A cloud of power

and shape that circled him and slowly began to lift Yeshua off the ground.

We all stood there, holding each other, and we watched our friend – the Master, the Lord, the Messiah – slowly disappear among the cloud until he was gone.

There was no fanfare. No grand goodbye. Just that swirling cloud around him as he was raised higher and higher.

And then, just like that, Yeshua was gone.

We were left staring up into the clouds above.

As we stood there, suddenly two angels appeared beside us.

'You Galileans! Why do you just stand here looking up at an empty sky?'

We all looked at each other in awed surprise. But with no paralysing fear anymore.

How strange, I thought, *that this is no longer strange.*

Then one of the angels spoke: 'This very Yeshua who was taken up from among you to heaven will come as certainly – and mysteriously – as he left.'

And with that, they too were gone.

We stood there, for I do not know how long. Lost in our thoughts. Of all that had occurred – and of all that lay ahead.

I felt no fear, only the powerful presence of our Lord within me. It was as if he had transcended from the sky right into our hearts.

My mind then raced back to something that Yeshua had once said to us. I could hear the words like it was yesterday.

He'd told us to be like salt – to add life and flavour to everything. To shine.

'You're here to be light, bringing out the God-colors in the world. God is not a secret to be kept.' His words were flooding back to me and I felt my heart race.

His light was not a secret to be kept.

'If I make you light-bearers, you don't think I'm going to hide you under a bucket, do you?' Yeshua always had a warm smile when talking like this. 'Now that I've put you there on a hilltop, on a light stand – shine! Keep open house; be generous with your lives . . .'

And right there he had given us our calling.

To me, these past few years had felt like time had been standing still. And only now was it beginning to tick again.

We stood a little longer, before eventually I noticed Kephas reach out and squeeze his brother's shoulder. It was time.

Time to depart. To begin.

Author's Note

This story is written from the perspective of the first eyewitnesses. I stuck closely to the accounts recorded in the four gospels, though some dialogue and other details have been added for context and flow.

However, not a single word of Yeshua has been changed from the original accounts in the New Testament. I have used different English translations to capture his words depending on the context, either from the NIV, MSG or ERV translations.

In writing a book like this, I also wanted to be authentic to the original setting and to avoid anglicised names that are over-familiar to many. The region in which Yeshua (Jesus) lived was complicated and remains contested to this day.

It is worth noting that throughout the Roman Empire at that time, Greek and Latin were the dominant languages. Yeshua himself was Jewish and would have read the Scriptures in Hebrew. However, as a Galilean, Yeshua's everyday language would have been Aramaic. The gospels preserve some of Jesus' most intimate words in Aramaic.

To be authentic, I've used a mixture of Greek, Hebrew and Aramaic names for people and places to reflect the social context of Yeshua's time.

I owe a huge thank you to Bible scholar Dr Andrew Ollerton for being a constant theological guide throughout the process of writing this book. A calm, clear voice – both spiritually and as a friend.

Also to Craig Borlase for helping with the early structure, tone and timing and to Andy Lyon for his editorial excellence and constant support and encouragement. And to Rabbi Jason Sobel, Dr Peter Williams from Tyndale House (Cambridge), and Dr Jesse Stone from the Come & See Foundation, for their theological guidance and cultural and naming insights. Also to Frank Harrison and Open Eyes for their endless kindness and generosity.

Part of the proceeds from this book are donated to charities supporting vulnerable people and communities around the world.

Please join us in praying that this book will bring many millions to know for themselves the truth that sets us free...

What Happened to the Disciples?

YOU HAVE BEEN reading in this book about the stories of a few of Jesus' disciples. The New Testament tells us what happened to two of them – Yudah of Kerioth (Judas Iscariot) and Yakov (James). But he had twelve in all. Other historical sources help us develop a picture of how the rest of them might have lived and died.

Kephas (Peter) – He became the leader of the early church, just as Jesus said would happen. He died by crucifixion, ordered by Emperor Nero. It is believed that he asked to be crucified upside down to distinguish his death from Jesus.

Yakov (James) – He was the first disciple to be martyred for his faith, around AD 44. He was executed by the sword under the orders of King Herod Agrippa I.

Yohanan (John) – He may have been the author of the Gospel of John, three letters (1, 2 and 3 John) and the book of Revelation. After Jesus' ascension, John played a significant role in the early Christian church, particularly in Ephesus. He was exiled to the island of Patmos, where he wrote Revelation. There were written suggestions of him being tortured with burning oil.

Andreas (Andrew) – He is thought to have travelled and preached in regions such as Scythia, Greece and Asia Minor. According to early Christian writings, Andrew's martyrdom came in Patras, Greece, where he was crucified on an X-shaped cross.

Philip – He travelled widely, including Phrygia in Asia Minor and Carthage in North Africa. His cause of death is unknown, although he is suspected to have been killed at the orders of a Roman proconsul who was enraged that his wife had converted to Christianity because of Philip's teaching.

Bartholomew/Nathanael – He travelled as far as India, Armenia, Ethiopia and Mesopotamia. His cause of death is unknown, although he is believed to have been beheaded or possibly skinned alive.

Levi (Matthew) – His background as a tax collector provided him with skills in record-keeping and writing, which would have proved useful when he wrote his account of Jesus' life – the Gospel of Matthew. (Although some claim this Gospel was written anonymously.) He is reported to have travelled to Ethiopia, Persia and Parthia. His cause of death is unknown, although he is suspected to have been stabbed.

Ta'om (Thomas) – He travelled eastward, possibly reaching as far as India. He is believed to have founded Christian communities and performed many miracles in the name of Jesus. He is believed to have been stabbed to death by four soldiers.

James the son of Clopas – He became a leader of the early church in Jerusalem. It is suspected his death was by stoning.

Shimon (Simon the Zealot) – According to tradition, Simon the Zealot preached in various regions, including Egypt, North Africa and Persia, where he is believed to have been martyred for his faith. It is thought he was killed after refusing to sacrifice to the sun god.

Judas Thaddaeus – His cause of death is unknown, although he is believed to have been shot with arrows.

Matthias – He was not originally one of the twelve apostles but had been a follower since the beginning. He was later chosen to replace Judas Iscariot after Judas' betrayal and subsequent death. He is thought to have preached in Cappadocia, the Caspian Sea area, and Ethiopia. He was sentenced to death by stoning.

Academics believe the average age of the disciples to be around 15 to 25 years old during the time they were with Jesus.

What Next?

To discover more about Yeshua (Jesus):

Try reading the New Testament Bible accounts of the life of Jesus in the Gospels of Matthew, Mark, Luke and John.

Alternatively, try:
The Bible Course www.thebiblecourse.org
or *Alpha* www.alpha.org.uk.
Or visit your local Christian church.

Some other books that have helped my journey of faith:

The Jesus I Never Knew by Philip Yancey
Beautiful Outlaw by John Eldredge
The Bible: A Story that Makes Sense of Life
by Andrew Ollerton
Mere Christianity by C. S. Lewis
Questions of Life by Nicky Gumbel
The Cross and the Lynching Tree by James H. Cone
The Ragamuffin Gospel by Brennan Manning
Messy Spirituality by Mike Yaconelli
The Purpose Driven Life by Rick Warren

Names of Jesus

Yeshua – Hebrew
Yasu – Arabic
Isho – Aramaic
Jesus – English

Meaning: He who saves . . .